DURABLES:

ARTICLES,

POEMS, AND

REVIEWS

LINDA L.

SCISSON

DURABLES:

ARTICLES,

POEMS, AND

REVIEWS

LINDA L.

SCISSON

DEDICATION

To those who walk their talk
and talk their walk

CONTENTS

ACKNOWLEDGMENTS

This collection of articles, poems, and reviews would not have happened without *Excel Online* Christian magazine, a publication of Fellowship Bible Church in Little Rock, Arkansas. I'm particularly indebted to the magazine's first editor, who became my first editor, Tracy Noble. Her encouraging words and wise edits were like apples of gold in settings of silver (Prov. 25:11).

I definitely remember my initial thoughts on submitting my first article to *Excel Online*. I came to a pretty fast conclusion that I could handle the rejection if my article were not accepted. After all, I was not a journalism or English major, and other than one poem in my state's newspaper decades ago, I was unpublished. With a "nothing ventured, nothing gained" attitude—which, I suppose, could be considered a mustard seed of faith—I hit the electronic-mail "Send" button with "Seeing Ourselves in Seabiscuit" as an attachment. That was Tuesday, August 5, 2003, at 12:18 AM. A month later, that pony galloped into cyberspace.

Fast forward to March 19, 2007, the day I received permission from Fellowship Bible Church to submit my articles (published between September 2003 and April 2006) elsewhere in "whatever way you would like to." Because of the church's generosity (releasing their "All Rights Reserved" designation back to me), the idea of getting my first book published became a probability, rather than a possibility.

Fifteen articles and poems that appeared in *Excel Online* are included here: A Box *and* a Dress; All in the Family; Baby Boy of Bethlehem;

Beautiful Swans; Blood, Sweat, and Tears; Celebrities; Daylight Saving Time; Downsizing; Our Founding Father; Pleasant Words; Seeing Ourselves in Seabiscuit; Table Manners; The Common Good; The Leaning Tower; and Truly, Truly. I have slightly edited a few of them to give a more generic voice.

As *Durables* contains forty-five pieces, I could list forty-five plus people who have contributed over the last five decades to my Christian growth and (directly or indirectly) with the writing of this book. I'm reminded of a quote by Leo Buscaglia: "Too often we underestimate the power of a touch, a smile, a kind word, a listening ear, an honest compliment, or the smallest act of caring, all of which have the potential to turn a life around." Thanks to all of you who have enriched my life with that kind of transforming power.

Finally, may I offer praise, glory, and honor to my Creator, Sustainer, and Strong Tower for His grace in taking *Durables* off its perch and giving it wings.

INTRODUCTION

Prior to having my manuscript turned into a book, I discovered the word *durable* in the Bible, and took that as a sign that my chosen title for a book that centers on Christianity was a suitable one.

"Riches and honor are with me; yea, *durable* riches and righteousness" (Prov. 8:18 KJV, emphasis added).

I also considered that a book in print has the potential to be a source of significance in one's life, for the reader and the writer. A book serves a purpose. It informs, it inspires, it befriends. As one turns the page, one's life may turn in a new direction.

Literally, one could say that a book in print is durable—"able to exist for a long time without significant deterioration" (*Merriam-Webster's Collegiate Dictionary. 11th ed.*). Yet, even with the best of technology, a book has a shelf life. It ages. It fades. It goes out of print. It does not last forever.

God's Word, however, stands forever (Isa. 40:8). It does not deteriorate. It does not change. It is a continuous lamp and light. The Word is with God. The Word is God (John 1:1).

It is my prayer that God's Word that I reference in *Durables* will give you a deeper knowledge, belief, and understanding (Isa. 43:10) of God's beauty, goodness, grace, love, and truth. God's attributes are more than durable in the singular sense. God's Word is living, active, and very sharp (Heb. 4:12). That denotes the plural sense, durables . . . with a shelf life that goes far beyond this earthly life. God's Word is boundless, timeless, infinite, everlasting, and eternal.

A Box *and* a Dress

The awe and wonder of childhood was richly demonstrated at Fellowship Bible Church in Little Rock, Arkansas, on the third Sunday morning in December of 2003. Teaching Pastor Bill Parkinson announced that he gave a Christmas gift to his three-year-old grand-daughter, Anna. With a keen sense of appreciation, the little girl pro-claimed, "Look! Grandpa gave me a box!" Promptly, Anna was told there was *more* to the gift than the box. There was something *inside* the box. And so, the three-year-old expanded her original thank you: "Look! Grandpa gave me a box *and* a dress!"

Like a generous grandparent, God wants to give. In the past, in the present, in the future, God is a grand giver. In John 3:16, we read: "For God so loved the world, that He *gave* His only begotten Son, that who-ever believes in Him should not perish, but have eternal life." In Luke 12:32, Jesus tells His disciples, "Do not be afraid, little flock, for your Father has chosen gladly to *give* you the kingdom." In Revelation 2:10, an angel speaking on behalf of Jesus says, "Be faithful until death, and I *will give* you the crown of life."

A gift requires a recipient. Without someone to *receive* a gift, it can be nothing more than an empty container—a box signifying nothing. As Robert Lewis told the congregation on December 21 in "Experiencing Bethlehem's Manger," when the Kingdom of God came down to earth, it was "like a free gift out of nowhere that changes everything." In order to receive this free gift, and apply its truth to my life, I have to take a journey. It's a journey in my head, "Come now, and let us reason together" (Isa. 1:18), and a journey in my heart, "Blessed are the pure in heart, for they shall see God" (Matt. 5:8).

In December 2003, a young girl appreciates a gift box as much as the dress inside. "Look! Grandpa gave me a box *and* a dress!" Perhaps she was imagining all the fun, creative things she could do with a box. In her mind, the box was as much as a gift as the dress. So, I reason that I must come to Jesus as a little child (Matt. 18:3), clothed in humility (1 Pet. 5:5), in order to receive the awesome gift of Jesus as my Savior.

Also, it is reasonable to thank God for all the gifts He gave me, He gives me, and He will give in the future. "Oh give thanks to the LORD, for He is good; for His lovingkindness is everlasting." That's found in Psalm 106:1 and is repeated at Psalm 107:1, Psalm 118:1, Psalm 118:29, and Psalm 136:1. After all, God is the ultimate philanthropist.

James 4:8 tells me to draw near to God and He will draw near to me. Did I get that? God, the grand giver of everything that is good (James 1:17), has the capacity and the desire to draw near to me. As I draw near to God and ask in faith for God's free gift of salvation, the best gift in the whole wide world, Jesus Christ becomes mine (1 Pet. 1:3-5). God comes to my rescue, and I discover—as Robert announced the Sunday before Christmas—"There's goodness in the world." As I build on opening my heart to Jesus Christ, I am changed. I am moved. I am resurrected. This box of my existence becomes a treasure: something—or rather—*someone* of significance. Christ in me, the hope of glory (Col. 1:27).

You bet, that three-year-old child was onto something as she thanked her Grandpa for a simple box. Like a budding prophetess, she knew the beauty of what God can do with a seemingly insignificant object. The box could be a doll's house, a dishwasher, or a desk. The box could be a computer, a continent, a xylophone, a purse. The box could be a prayer closet. Like the birth of Jesus, the box was "like a free gift out of nowhere that changes everything."

Did Anna already know these possibilities—the true meaning of transformation?

In a matter of months, will she learn of Moses, who turned from being a slave to a deliverer of thousands of people held in bondage? Of Gideon, who turned from hiding wheat in a winepress to leading God's handpicked army to victory? Of David, who turned from being a shepherd to a fighter and king of a nation? Of Peter, who turned from denying Jesus three times to boldly proclaiming Jesus many times? Will the child soon discover the change that occurred in Mary? Who at a tender age said a resounding "Yes!" to God's plan, humbly proclaiming, "Behold, the handmaid of the Lord; be it unto me according to thy Word" (Luke 1:38 KJV).

Did Anna know that her little act of obedience—giving thanks for a mere box—would fit in with something else God wants to do in other people's lives? The brief remarks of a three-year-old "teacher" certainly brought spiritual insight to this "beyond fifty-three-year-old."

"Out of the mouth of babes and sucklings hast thou ordained strength . . . " (Ps. 8:2 KJV).

Had God already implanted in the little girl's mind that she, like the child Jesus, must "be busy about my Father's business"? (Luke 2:49). After all, ". . . life is about letting God use you for His purposes, not your using Him for your own purpose." (Warren, Rick. *The Purpose-Driven Life*)

Did the child know that God could take a tiny gesture of goodness and magnify the results? With only five loaves of bread and two fish, Jesus miraculously fed over five thousand (Matt. 14:17-20).

Did the little girl know that God could do wonders with a thankful heart? As Bible teacher Beth Moore said, "The more we applaud Him, the more He comes back for an encore."

From manger to majesty: the baby Jesus—born in a box, wrapped in narrow strips of cloth—becomes the King of Kings, the Lord of lords, the name above all names, dressed in splendor, dressed in strength whose train of His robe fills the temple (Isa. 6:1). Three-year-old Anna, filled with joy over a box and a dress from Grandpa, must have known—with her divine imagination and pure heart —"in Him we live and move and have our being, . . ." (Acts 17:28 NKJV).

A Pearl of Great Value

Have you heard the parable about the pearl? A merchant seeking pearls finds one of great value, and he leaves it where he found it. He thinks he is not good enough to take it. At some point in his life, his self esteem had shattered. (*"Can any good thing come out of . . . ?"* John 1:46). So, the merchant dismisses the idea of taking, as his own, "one pearl of great value" (Matt. 13:46).

That's not what it says in the Bible. What our sacred text actually says: ". . . a merchant seeking fine pearls, and upon finding one pearl of great value, he went and sold all that he had and bought it" (Matt. 13:45-46).

The passage is a parable: "a . . . story that illustrates a moral attitude or a religious principle" (*Merriam-Webster's Collegiate Dictionary, 11th ed.*). As in other stories, Jesus spoke this parable to describe what it is like to seek and find "the kingdom of heaven" (Matt. 13:45).

Taking Matthew 13:45-46 in pieces, I see the following:

(1) The merchant seeks *fine pearls* and *finds one pearl of great value*. The merchant does not look for a button for his shirt or a battery for his watch. He does not look for the ordinary, he looks for the extraordinary. He does not search for jagged and blemished pearls; he searches for smooth and iridescent pearls. And he finds one flawless gem of great value.

(2) The merchant *went*. After finding the "one pearl of great value" (Matt. 13:47), the merchant did not stay where he was. He got up. He moved from one place to another place. He took a leap of faith. There

was more to do now that he had found the rare and beautiful, the choice and precious.

(3) The merchant *sold all* that he had. He did not throw his possessions away. He did not trade them in for other things. He sold them. He did not sell part of what he had; he sold everything. Don't you imagine some of the things he sold were of value to him? Things that he had kept for a long time? Things that had occupied a great deal of his time or thought? He sold everything—from material possessions to character defects (Mark 4:19; 1 John 2:16)—that held him back from keeping the "one pearl of great value" (Matt. 13:46).

(4) The merchant sold all *that he had*. He did not sell himself. He did not lower his standards. He did not become a slave under a harsh taskmaster. Nor did he allow himself to become another's god or idol (Isa. 2:22). Nor did he lose his God-given personality during the course of the selling spree. Quite the contrary: His true self blossomed, as he gained a healthier perspective on life by aligning himself with the Giver of Life (John 12:24-26).

(5) The merchant *bought* the pearl. He did not borrow it to display on special occasions. He did not put it on layaway. He did not steal it. He bought it.

> "The kingdom of heaven is like a merchant seeking fine pearls,
> and upon finding one pearl of great value, he went and sold all
> that he had and bought it" (MATT. 13:45-46).

From biblical days to modern days, a pearl represents something of value. For instance, Jonathan Janson notes that Dutch artist Johannes Vermeer (1632-1675) often portrayed women wearing pearls, one of them being "The Girl with a Pearl Earring." In this oil on canvas, Vermeer enlarged the size of a drop or tear shaped pearl in order "to adorn the girl with something spectacular." The pearl is out of proportion, as the artist either painted an artificial pearl or he exaggerated its dimensions—to make it look like an immense pearl.

In God's holy city, there is a spectacular pearl out of proportion to anything we have ever seen on earth (Rev. 21:12, 21). Followers of Jesus Christ, at some point after our earthly death, will see a tremendous gate of "a single pearl."

> "It [the holy city, Jerusalem, coming down out of heaven] had a great and high wall, with twelve gates . . . And the twelve gates were twelve pearls; each one of the gates was a *single pearl*" (REV. 21:12, 21, EMPHASIS ADDED).

Isn't that interesting? In Matthew (the first book in the New Testament), Jesus describes himself as "one pearl of great value" (Matt. 13:46). And in Revelation (the last book), we read that each one of twelve gates is comprised of "a single pearl" (Rev. 21:21).

By definition, a "gate" is "an opening in a wall or fence." It is "a means of entrance or exit" (*Merriam-Webster's*). God could have placed the magnificent pearl in another part of His holy city. He placed the pearl at the gateway.

Jesus represents the pearl in the passages from Matthew and Revelation. Jesus is our means of entrance into eternal life. "One pearl of great value" is spoken about *by* Jesus and is *about* Jesus (Matt. 13:46). And a literal pearl of huge dimensions stands at the entrance to each gate of God's holy city (Rev. 21:21).

The good news: followers of Jesus Christ, one day, will pass through a gate comprised of a breath-taking "single pearl" and live forever in "the kingdom of heaven" with Jesus, The One Pearl of Great Value. We are given a life in heaven—that stretches forever and ever—as a valuable gift through our acceptance of Jesus Christ as our Savior and Lord, who paid the price to make this possible (2 Cor. 5:21). And that, in turn, makes you and me, in the sight of our God, a pearl of great value (1 Pet. 2:4-6).

A Sweet Communion

3

On the third day there was a wedding in Cana of Galilee, and the mother of Jesus was there; and both Jesus and His disciples were invited to the wedding. When the wine ran out, the mother of Jesus said to Him, "They have no wine." And Jesus said to her, "Woman, what does that have to do with us? My hour has not yet come." His mother said to the servants, "Whatever He says to you, do it." Now there were six stone water pots set there for the Jewish custom of purification, containing twenty or thirty gallons each.

Jesus said to them, "Fill the water pots with water." So they filled them up to the brim. And He said to them, "Draw some out now and take it to the headwaiter." So they took it to him. When the headwaiter tasted the water which had become wine, and did not know where it came from (but the servants who had drawn the water knew), the headwaiter called the bridegroom, and said to him, "Every man serves the good wine first, and when the people have drunk freely, then he serves the poorer wine; but you have kept the good wine until now." This beginning of His signs Jesus did in Cana of Galilee, and manifested His glory, and His disciples believed in Him (JOHN 2:1-11).

Why was turning water into wine considered a manifestation of the glory of Jesus Christ, as we read in John 2:11? After all, magicians back in Bible times performed supernatural feats beyond the ordinary experiences of life (Exod. 7:22).

First, let's look at the word, "glory." The Amplified Bible says by this first miracle or "wonderwork," Jesus "displayed His greatness and His power openly" (John 2:11 AMP). So, we can describe "glory" as "greatness" and "power."

Secondly, I believe Exodus 4 ("Moses Given Powers") foreshadows John 2 ("Miracle at Cana") and brings insight into the question at hand: why was turning water into wine considered a manifestation of Jesus' glory?

In Exodus 4:9, God speaks to Moses about performing a miracle in the context of Pharaoh's reluctance to let the Israelites out of Egypt:

> ". . . you [Moses] shall take some water from the Nile and pour
> it on the dry ground; and the water which you take from the
> Nile will become blood on the dry ground"
> (EXOD. 4:9; SEE ALSO 7:17).

In John 2:7, Jesus commanded that water be placed in six water pots, which were used for the Jewish custom of purification. Then Jesus miraculously turned the water into wine.

Note that water is the transporting tool in Exodus 4:9 and John 2:6-11. In the Old Testament, Moses is instructed by God to take water from the Nile and pour it on the dry ground, and the water will become blood. In the New Testament, Jesus is instructed by God, with His mother's prompting, to take water from "holy" water pots and pour it out among the people, and the water becomes wine.

See some similarities?

First, could we safely say that Moses is a foreshadow symbol of Jesus?

Secondly, it's generally recognized that in Bible times the Nile River symbolized life itself. Later, in an outdoor setting, Jesus confidently says to a thirsty woman that He is the provider of *"living* water" (John 4:10, emphasis added).

Thirdly, the water pots were symbols of purification, being used in religious washing ceremonies. Could we safely connect life in its fullness ("filled to the brim") and purity here, especially in context of the entire Bible?

Fourth similarity: the water became blood in the Book of Exodus, and the water became wine in the Book of John. Isn't wine, or the fruit of the vine, a symbol of the blood of Jesus Christ that "takes away the sin of the world"? (John 1:29). Again, I'm sensing a biblical link—a sweet communion—between abundant life and purity.

Notice in John 2:7, Jesus told the servants to "fill the water pots with water." The servants "filled them up to the brim." Back then, a wedding party lasted a whole week with lots of people and lots to eat and drink, however drunkenness was "a great disgrace" (Isa. 5:11; Prov. 20:1, 23:29-35). (According to William Barclay, they actually drank their wine in a mixture composed of two parts of wine to three parts of water.) It was also a social disgrace to run out of wine at a wedding.

How did Jesus' turning water into wine reveal His glory, greatness, and power? Let's glance at events prior to the wedding. Before beginning His public ministry, Jesus had been in the desert where He was severely tempted by the devil (Matt. 4). Soon thereafter, Jesus appears at this village wedding (John 2:1-11), where the custom was the newly married couple, wearing crowns and dressed in royal robes, opened their home to receive guests for an entire week. Barclay notes, "They were treated like a king and queen, were actually addressed as king and queen, and their word was law." As His gift to the bride and groom, Jesus turned over one hundred gallons of water into wine.

In closing, I turn to Henry H. Halley (*Halley's Bible Handbook: An Abbreviated Bible Commentary*) to offer, what I believe is, the best response to the question: "Why was turning water into wine considered a manifestation of Jesus' glory?" As we read it, whether we are wine abstainers or partakers, let's lift the cup of salvation in praise to our Lord (Ps. 116:13; Luke 22:20). And drink from the river of His delights (Ps. 36:8).

Significance of this miracle: Jesus had just submitted himself, for forty days, to every suggestion Satan was capable of offering, as to how He should use His miraculous powers, and had steadfastly refused to use them for His own personal need. Then [Jesus moves] from the wilderness directly to the wedding. And though His subsequent miracles were wrought largely to relieve suffering, this first miracle was done at a wedding feast, on a festive occasion, ministering to human joy, making people happy as if Jesus wanted to announce, right at the start, that the religion which He was now introducing into the world was no religion of asceticism [strict self-denial], but a religion of natural joy. It was Jesus' blessing on marriage.

All in the Family

Is there a biblical name on your family tree? I've discovered an "Elisha" on mine, and that makes me want to know more about my great grandfather, as well as his namesake, the prophet Elisha.

Elisha Stuard Keathley was born September 8, 1849, in Gibson County, Tennessee. He died July 25, 1929, in Danville (Yell County), Arkansas. Elisha and his wife, Eliza Jane McCarrell Keathley, had seven children: four boys and three girls, one of whom was my paternal grandmother, Arvie Zelia Keathley Scisson (1888-1979). A handwritten entry in my grandmother's Bible credits my great, great grandparents, Arch Keathley and Arvie Caraway Branch Keathley, for naming their son Elisha.

The Bible credits Shaphat of Abel-meholah for naming his son Elisha, which means "God is Savior." Elisha was a disciple and "double portion" successor of the prophet Elijah. Elisha (similar in spelling to Elijah) held the prophetic office for a stunning fifty-five years (1 Kings 19:16-19; 2 Kings 2:1-15; Luke 4:27).

One story about Elisha that is packed with insight is 2 Kings 5. Yet the main, visible character is not Elisha, but Naaman, who has everything going for him except one thing: he has leprosy.

In God's sovereignty, two women are chosen to set Naaman's healing into motion. First, a servant girl speaks to Naaman's wife, who in turn speaks to Naaman. What is the servant girl's compassionate plea? "If only my master would see the prophet who is in Samaria! He would cure him of his leprosy" (2 Kings 5:2-3 NIV).

A few verses later, we read that Naaman, a great army commander, "went with his horses and chariots and stopped at the door of Elisha's house" (2 Kings 5:9 NIV). The instructions, by way of a messenger that Elisha sends to the door, are clear: For Naaman to be cured, he is to *wash himself seven times in the Jordan River* (2 Kings 5:10).

That is not what Naaman wants to hear. Dipping seven times in the Jordan is not the news he expects. Naaman prefers a simple solution; an instant healing, a quick fix. He falsely presumes Elisha, the man of God, would "surely come out to me and stand and call on the name of the LORD his God, wave his hand over the spot and cure me of my leprosy" (2 Kings 5:11 NIV). You see, Naaman wants God on Naaman's terms.

Not only is Naaman unhappy about the method of healing, he does not like the chosen location. Not the Jordan River, Naaman complains, but "Abana and Pharpar" as those are "better" rivers. Pride and presumption overtake Naaman, and so "he turned and went off in a rage"—with his loathsome leprosy (2 Kings 5:12).

For Naaman's sake and for our sake, God is merciful (Ps. 86:15; Luke 1:50). He offers Naaman a second chance. This time, God turns to other trusted servants to try to persuade Naaman to follow Elisha's instructions. The servants say, ". . . if the prophet had told you to do some great thing, would you not have done it? How much more, then, when he tells you, 'Wash and be cleansed'!" (2 Kings 5:13 NIV).

Fortunately, Naaman humbles himself and obeys. He chooses to follow God's instructions, as spoken through the prophet Elisha. What happens? Nothing short of a miracle; nothing short of the tender mercies of God: ". . . his flesh was restored and became clean like that of a young boy" (2 Kings 5:14 NIV).

We're all in the family (Eph. 3:15; Isa. 51:1-2). We're all created in the image of God. But we are the creatures, not the Creator; the clay, not the Potter (Rom. 9:21). So let's avoid taking for granted how God will work in a situation. Let's not presume upon our Holy Father. Let's not put God in a box. Let's accept His instructions: even if the message is unusual; even if the messenger is unexpected.

PRAYER

We praise You, Father God (Ps. 150:6). We confess we have made false presumptions. Forgive us, Lord, when we disregard Your chosen messengers, rather than hear and apply Your message as spoken through them. Thank You that "the truth will make us free" (John 8:32). Gracious God, deliver us from pettiness and pride and wrong thinking (Eph. 4:17-18). May we respect and reverence You and Your creation. May we discern Your trusted servants and obey them (Matt. 7:15-17; Heb. 13:17). May we trust in Your ways, rather than cling to our own understanding (Prov. 3:5-6, 21:2). In the name of Jesus: "the name which is above every name" (Phil. 2:9). Amen.

Angels in the Huddle

When our favorite football team scores the winning touchdown in the last second of the game, we sports fans are quick to show our emotions. We hop from our seats, and we hoot and holler, as it's obvious: we have seen an exciting event with a successful finish. Whether we witness the victory from the stands, hear it on the radio, or watch it on TV, we are thrilled when our team wins. And we're about to have a rip-roaring, good time.

Over two thousand years ago, an event on a hill called Calvary had all the appearance of a major defeat. If we could look through binoculars back in time, we would see a man on a cross. His name is Jesus. We can hardly recognize Him as His body is badly torn. There are external and internal injuries. Death is imminent. Dejection is written on the faces of the few friends standing by (John 19:25). Tears flow from a young mother's eyes, as she watches her son about to die, as insults from the rulers and soldiers hurl upon Jesus (Luke 23:35-36). We see the disciple, John, in shock, as he consoles Mary, the mother of Jesus (John 19:26-27). None of them understand. All are consumed by grief and doubt.

I imagine they say to themselves, "Jesus, who claimed to be 'the Christ, the Son of the living God' (Matt. 16:16-17); Jesus, who claimed to be 'one with the Father' (John 10:30); Jesus, who claimed to be the 'Son of Man' (Luke 6:5); is being crucified before our very eyes. Was He *not* who He said He was?"

Hold on, folks. Hold on. "The foolishness of God is wiser than man's wisdom, and the weakness of God is stronger than man's strength" (1 Cor. 1:25).

Like an unstoppable, All-American quarterback in the last second of a title game, God himself is the one running the ball on the all-important, final snap. And this play requires heavenly footwork, discipline, and the willingness to sacrifice. To put it mildly, this is high drama on Calvary Hill. Pep rallies, tailgate parties, and marching bands pale in comparison with this event. Let's pick it up, sports fans, as angels in the huddle are begging to tell:

Archie, Lead Angel in the Huddle: "I'll spread a thick blanket over the sun. That's my assignment. God told me to get it totally dark when Jesus dies on the cross. The sun is not to shine for three hours. So, I'm to spread quite a quilt over sunshine from noon to three (Matt. 27:45). Count on me. Got it covered."

Seeker, Second Angel in the Huddle: "Why's that?"

Archie, Lead Angel: "Because God said so. Isn't that reason enough? God said it ought to catch humankind's attention. Besides, when the lights are out, when everything's dark, no one can work. Maybe God's sports fans need a reminder that they don't have to work for their salvation; it's a gift. There's no fancy footwork for the human team to play, because Jesus does the work, supernaturally, taking on the dark death of sin for them."

Ripple, Third Angel: "You said it, Ang'! I got my orders from headquarters, too. Let me run it by you. I'm part of the wing formation. I'm to see that the curtain in the temple 'tears in two from top to bottom' (Matt. 27:51 NIV). Right? Or is your name Archangel?"

Archie, Lead Angel: "Wing formation or wishbone . . . whatever. The curtain's the job, Rip. And my name is Archangel. It's from my Father's side of the family."

Mercy Me, Fourth Angel: "Hear, hear, Mercy Me, at God's service! R-r-r-r-ready for a touchdown! I know what I do: I go shake the earth (Matt. 27:51). God's wide receiver, Isaiah, had a corner on that one: 'Oh, that You would rend the heavens! That You would come down! That the mountains might shake at Your presence'" (Isa. 64:1 NKJV).

Rocky, Fifth Angel: "Mercy Me, we're in for a sweep! While you shake, I split the rocks (Matt. 27:51). That reminds me of 'sharper than any two-edged sword' (Heb. 4:12), lined up at Luke 19:39-40. You know, when the Pharisees demanded Jesus to rebuke the disciples. And

Jesus answered back: 'I tell you that if these [disciples] should keep silent, the stones would immediately cry out'" (Luke 19:40 NKJV).

Sensible, Sixth Angel: "I can hear those rocks crying out as they split."

Archie, Lead Angel: "Truly, truly. No wonder Jesus is called the 'rock of salvation'" (Ps. 89:26 KJV).

Sensible, Sixth Angel: "Yeah, and He has authority over all of us little rocks" (Mark 1:22 KJV).

Archie, Lead Angel: "Good for you, Sense. Now, who's in charge of the 'Hail Mary'? You know, the code name involving the bodies of the saints?"

Believe-It-Or-Not, Seventh Angel: "I am. Here's how it's drawn up in the locker room: The tombs will open, and many bodies of the saints who had fallen asleep will rise. And coming out of the tombs after His resurrection, they will enter the holy city and appear to many" (Matt. 27:52).

Archie, Lead Angel: "Okay. The moment Jesus dies and shortly thereafter, here's the plan: Pitch dark for three hours in the afternoon. The curtain tears from top to bottom. The earth shakes. The rocks split. Tombs are opened. By the way, in over-time, Word is out we'll help pull off the Resurrection, as described at the Gospel According to Mark, chapter 16."

Seeker, Second Angel [looking toward the sidelines]: "Got to take a break for some 'living water' (John 4:10 KJV). Arch, could you tell me the purpose of all this sudden flurry of activity?"

Archie, Lead Angel: "Sure, Seeker. It's this message to humankind: On a hill called Calvary, Jesus dies with a number of strange occurrences going on. For one: the rip-roaring curtain that God has one of you help out on—Ripple, I believe it is: That curtain symbolizes Jesus' body, torn and ripped to pave the way for humankind's sins to be forgiven. Like a quarterback running through an unexpected hole in the line that points him straight to the goal post, men and women can now enter into a holy place with God, a previously restricted area, thanks to Jesus (2 Cor. 5:21).

"Before this event, God could not look down on sin, as God is too holy. That is, He could not look down on humankind: just too many personal fouls, interference, and being offside for our sky-high God to watch. Yet, the big, burly barrier has been removed by Jesus' work on the cross."

Seeker, Second Angel: "Like Jesus sacks sin?"

Archie, Lead Angel: "You got it! Compared to a never-ending agony of defeat in a literal hell (Mark 9:47-48), those with a glow-in-the-dark ticket to heaven are in store for a rip-roaring, good time. Because God has a gate, section, row, and seat reserved for them (John 14:2). And that news gives the earthlings a lot of up-field momentum (Ps. 150).

"So, angels in the huddle, on 'Hut 1, 2, 3,' before you fly off on your by-and-by assignments, pause on the top bleachers. Ask the broadcasters to speak through their microphones, and cheerleaders to shout through their megaphones, and marching bands to play on their trumpets and trombones: That Jesus Christ lived on earth dedicated to a mission. He came to save the lost. He came to die for our sins. He came to offer new life to all who are willing to receive Him (John 3:3; Matt. 7:21); to die to our former self (Matt. 3:11); and to be transformed by the renewing of our mind (Rom. 12:2).

"Finally, angels, take note of the last words of Jesus in a group setting to his diehard fans: 'I have told you these things, so that in Me, you may have peace. In this world you will have trouble. But take heart! I have overcome the world'" (John 16:33 NIV).

Seeker, Second Angel: "Uh, Archie. [Pause] I'm just part of the secondary. Could you run that past me, again?"

Archie, Lead Angel: "You bet, Seek. Jesus says to His disciples: 'I have told you these things so that in Me you may have perfect peace and confidence. In the world you have tribulation and trials and distress and frustration; but be of good cheer—take courage, be confident, certain, undaunted—for I have overcome the world. —I have deprived it of power to harm, have conquered it [for you]'" (John 16:33 AMP).

Angels in the Huddle: Archie, Seeker, Ripple, Mercy Me, Rocky, Sensible, and Believe-It-Or-Not (in unison and spontaneously, as they repeat a familiar phrase): "Holy, holy, holy, Lord God Almighty, who was, and is, and is to come" (Rev. 4:8 KJV).

Baby Boy of Bethlehem

Baby Boy of Bethlehem,
Is it true what they say?
You've come to save the world,
Not to judge it.
To heal the sick
And lift the broken hearted.

Baby Boy of Bethlehem,
Is it true what they say?
Your name is above every name.
You're Wonderful Counselor,
King of Kings, Lord of lords,
Prince of peace.

Baby Boy of Bethlehem,
Is it true what they say?
You will be misunderstood,
Beaten and betrayed, nailed to a cross.
And what will You say? "Forgive them,
Father, for they know not what they do."

Baby Boy of Bethlehem,
Is it true what they say?
On a day and an hour

No one on earth knows when
You will return
In the clouds with power and glory.

Baby Boy of Bethlehem
Be it so true—and I
Will offer You
More than gold, incense, and myrrh.
I'll cradle You in my arms,
I'll sing a lullaby of praise.

Baby Boy of Bethlehem,
Be it so true—and I
Will lay my burdens down.
I'll walk away from death.
I'll run to Your Father and say,
"Oh, I'm related to the Baby Boy of Bethlehem."

Beautiful Swans

Did you know there has been a sighting of swans at church? Not one or two, but a flock of swans. What is further unique: the church encourages more swans to find themselves a nest here. This is headlines: Swans Have Been Sighted!

Metaphorically, throughout literature swans embody what is beautiful. Take these examples: (1) Tchaikovsky's ballet, *Swan Lake*, where the lead swan wearing a crown becomes a beautiful maiden; (2) Wagner's opera, *Lohengrin*, where a knight arrives on a magical swan-boat; (3) White's book, *The Trumpet of the Swan*, where a beautiful, voiceless swan receives a trumpet, (4) Yeats' poem, "The Wild Swans at Coole," where "those brilliant creatures" are "mysterious, beautiful"; and (5) Hans Christian Andersen's story, *The Ugly Duckling*, where a duckling discovers his true identity as a swan with the declaration: "I never knew there was such happiness as this."

Who am I speaking of, literally, as "beautiful swans" seen here and there around the Lord's house? Those who are baptized in the faith (Matt. 28:19; Acts 2:38-41): men and women who take the plunge, as Jesus himself did in the Jordan River when he was thirty years old; men and women who show through their baptism the death, burial, and resurrection of Jesus Christ and their decision to trust Him as their Savior (Rom. 6:3-4). They have come to see, as I have, that abundant life may be summarized in seven words: "Christ in me, the hope of glory" (Col. 1:27).

When I was 34 years old, I was baptized by immersion. I wanted to go down into the water and come up out of it—soaking wet. I wanted my heart cleansed of sin and my body "washed with pure water" (Heb. 10:22). I wanted to symbolically be buried in Christ's death and resurrected as a new creation in Christ (Rom. 6:3-4). My Jordan River was Lake Nixon on June 2, 1985. Needless to say, my baptism-as-an-adult remains a milestone in my spiritual journey.

> "If anyone is in Christ, he is a new creation;
> the old has gone, the new has come!" (2 COR. 5:17 NIV).

Are you a beautiful swan? If "yes," do you realize that we are headline news to the Creator and sustainer of life? We are a royal priesthood. We are a peculiar people. We are a chosen generation—for God's own possession (1 Pet. 2:9). Let me express that another way: We are saints (Col. 1:11-13). According to Oswald Chambers, in *My Utmost for His Highest*, saints have a "genuine, living relationship with Jesus Christ" and "unrestrained devotion to Him" regardless of our circumstances. We are not gray and gangling in the sight of our God. We are not awkward or graceless. We are not ugly ducklings. We are beautiful swans.

Why did God lavish all this VIP treatment upon us? So that we "may declare the praises of Him" who called us "out of darkness into His wonderful light" (1 Pet. 2:9 NIV). We are the people of God. We have received mercy (1 Pet. 2:10). Like swans upon the brimming water, we are beautiful. And that's something to honk about.

> "Go . . . and tell the people the full message of this new life"
> (ACTS 5:20 NIV).

Birds from God's Perch

Have you ever wondered, how does a woodpecker absorb the shock of drilling a hole in a tree? Zap-zap-zap-zap-zap. . . . What prevents the woodpecker from getting a migraine headache? Or getting knocked out from all that drilling?

God provides. He created a sponge-like pad between the woodpecker's bill and its head to absorb the shock. This is a fact I learned in *God's Story*, a Bible study on the first 11 chapters of Genesis by Anne Graham Lotz that I took in 2005. It was an illustration to show that God is active in His creation in many ways.

Another example of God's unique activity among our feathered friends: God created at least one million barbs per feather on each bird. These barbs "act like zippers so that when the bird preens himself, he locks his feathers together." In rain or shine, this helps the bird. Lotz continues, "When it rains, he's waterproof. Or when he flies, the wind catches under his wings and he can stay up in the air."

The Bible makes over three hundred references to birds, naming more than twenty-five species, including—among others—the dove, eagle, raven, and sparrow. God created birds on the fifth day of creation (Gen. 1:21), and there are several biblical examples of how birds benefit our lives. Two examples:

(1) After a devastating flood, Noah waits to see if a dove that he had released from the ark would return with evidence, such as a leaf or twig, that the waters had receded (Gen. 8:8-11).

(2) In 1 Kings, during a season of drought, a raven brings Elijah

bread and meat near a brook east of the Jordan River; and this unique "food delivery service" was clearly commanded by the LORD (1 Kings 17:3-6).

Birds are mentioned in poetic terms, too. At the Jordan River, immediately following His baptism, Jesus "saw the Spirit of God descending as a dove and lighting on Him" (Matt. 3:16). In Psalm 124, we read: "Our soul has escaped as a bird out of the snare of the trapper" (Ps. 124:7a NKJV). There is good news, too, in Luke 12 where we are told that we "are more valuable than many sparrows" (Luke 12:7). And there's an eagle simile in Isaiah 40: "Those who wait for the LORD will gain new strength; they will mount up with wings like eagles . . ." (Isa. 40:31).

I recall two bird encounters that were helpful in my spiritual journey. In May 1983, I attended a weekend conference on Petit Jean Mountain in Morrilton, Arkansas. While I had been invited by one of the speakers, I had only recently met her and the other participants were hardly acquaintances. After the first day of migrating my way through new places and new faces, I considered skipping the remaining sessions, driving home, and chalking it all up to experience.

I walked out of the retreat center, sat on a bench, and gazed upon the beautiful mountains as I contemplated my decision. I told God I felt like a bull in a china shop, and I thought it was time to quietly pack my bags and go home. Suddenly, a huge bird flew overhead, coming so close to me that I ducked. I interpreted this encounter as a sign from God that I should stay.

I'm glad I did: That evening, May 6, 1983, I experienced a filling of the Holy Spirit (Acts 2:33; Rom. 8:9-11) that remains a significant "memorial stone" (Josh. 4:7) in my spiritual journey. In fact, seven days later, I had my first experience of speaking in tongues (1 Cor. 12:10), which I believe was directly linked to the prayers spoken over me a week earlier on the mountain top.

A parenthetical note on speaking in tongues: Any gift from God, like any truth from God, can be used for God's glory or misused for other reasons, such as trying to enhance my own importance. With that said, may I offer that speaking in tongues, on occasion, has added a measure of beauty and depth, mystery and sweetness to my conversations with

God or praises to God. I hasten to add the significance that I find in the placement of the spiritual gifts. They are found in 1 Corinthians 12 and 14. Sandwiched in between is chapter 13, which is termed "the most excellent way," the way of love.

Fast forward to the summer of 2000. I found an injured sparrow lying on the ground, so I ran into the house for a cardboard box and shovel, with the idea I would take the bird to the veterinarian. As I slowly approached the sparrow and gently brought the shovel close underneath his body, he hobbled a few feet away. I was crushed in spirit. In a rather frantic tone of voice, I spoke to my broken-winged sparrow: "If you don't let me help you, you're not going to make it."

Like my injured and frightened bird, who eventually allowed me to take him to a place of recovery, do we allow God to help us? Not only help us one time, but many times through the wingspan of our lives? Or do we hobble away in fear or strut away in pride? I think of what must have been a frantic, but nurturing tone of our Lord's voice as Jesus spoke to an unbelieving city: "How often I wanted to gather your children together, as a hen gathers her brood under her wings, but you were not willing!" (Luke 13:34b NKJV).

When it becomes difficult to absorb the shocks and surprises of life, may we "take refuge in the shelter" of God's wings (Ps. 61:4). For in all kinds of weather, God is actively involved. He is the God who bears us up "on eagles' wings" and brings us to himself (Exod. 19:4). And, as Civilla D. Martin writes, He is the God whose "eye is on the sparrow, and I know He watches me."

Blood, Sweat, and Tears

I wanted
to write You,
Lord Jesus, a lofty
Easter poem. I can't.
I did not see the curtain
tear in two from top to bottom.
I did not see the earth shake, the rocks
split apart, the graves break open, the land
at noon cover with darkness. I've never sweated

blood in the Garden
at Gethsemane. I've never
been nailed to a cross on a hill at
Calvary, or buried in a tomb and risen
in three days. I've never taken on the sins
of the world, or ascended to the heavens, or seen
the face of God. I've never sat to the right of a throne
surrounded by thousands of angels. Maybe that's the reason,
for the life of me, I can't write a poem on Easter to someone like You.

10 Celebrities

My father shouts the celebrity's name clear across the room. In a hotel lobby in St. Louis, Missouri, Dad even persuades those on a crowded elevator to stop the door from closing. Some forty years ago, there was no way my Dad was going to be stopped from getting his three kids the autograph of baseball's legendary Willie Mays. I remember the moment as though it were yesterday.

Doesn't our Heavenly Father make a determined effort to get *our* autograph? Aren't we, as God's creations, so special to Him that, in a strong sense of the word, our heavenly Dad would interrupt us—often through the circumstances of our lives—and ask us to sign on with Him and His Plan for our life? Aren't we God's celebrities, to the extent that God would grant us *His* autograph—by way of The Holy Bible—that not only reveals His names, but also His attributes and His promises?

As in a baseball game after hitting a home run, let's swing around the bases and see a few scriptures that back up the fact that we are God's celebrities.

FIRST BASE
"Before I formed you in the womb I knew you . . ." (Jer. 1:5).

SECOND BASE
"Indeed, the very hairs of your head are all numbered. Do not fear; you are more valuable than many sparrows" (Luke 12:7).

THIRD BASE

"You are a letter of Christ, cared for by us, written not with ink but with the Spirit of the living God, not on tablets of stone but on tablets of human hearts" (2 Cor. 3:3).

To many people, Willie Howard Mays, Jr., born May 6, 1931, is known as the "Say Hey Kid." It was like a new name for him once he excelled in baseball. Once we, as followers of Jesus Christ, overcome the trials and temptations the world, the flesh, and the devil offer, we too will be given a new name. In fact our sacred text promises that followers of Jesus Christ who remain "faithful until death" (Rev. 2:10) will be given more (much more) than a new name. And that brings us to . . .

HOME PLATE

Revelation, chapters 2 and 3 reveal:

To those "celebrities" who overcome: God will give the crown of life, a morning star, white garments, hidden manna, and authority over the nations with a ruler's rod of iron.

To those "celebrities" who overcome: God will grant permission to eat of the tree of life in heaven, permission to walk with Jesus Christ, and permission to sit down with Jesus on His throne.

To those "celebrities" who overcome: God promises that He will *not* erase the overcomer's name from the Book of Life, and that the overcomer will *not* be hurt by the second death. God promises that Jesus Christ will confess the overcomer's name before God and His angels, and that God will keep the overcomer from the hour of testing. God also promises that the overcomer will be made "a pillar in the temple" of God, and the overcomer "will not go out from it anymore" (Rev. 3:12).

To those "celebrities" who overcome: Jesus Christ will write on the overcomer "the name of My God, and the name of the city of My God, the new Jerusalem, which comes down out of heaven from My God, and My new name" (Rev. 3:12).

To those "celebrities" who overcome: The Son of God will give the overcomer "a white stone, and a new name written on the stone which no one knows but he who receives it" (Rev. 2:17). And, by the way, this "new name" was prophesied by Isaiah: ". . . and thou shalt be called by a new name, which the mouth of the LORD shall name" (Isa. 62:2 KJV).

"A new name"—that no one knows but the individual receiving it. Not hastily written by hand with a lead pencil on a scratch sheet of paper. But "a new name" engraved by the hand of God on "a white stone," promised centuries ago to those who overcome; that is, to those who remain "faithful until death" (Rev. 2:10). "A new name" not written outside a crowded elevator among devoted baseball fans, but written inside heaven surrounded by angels and close to streets of gold and gates of pearls (Rev. 21:12, 21).

We are God's "Say Hey Kids" (John 1:12) in the center field of God's sacred heart. God knows our names twenty-four hours of each and every day. That fact gives reason to pause and sign on with the Psalmist, who must have known something significant about undistracted devotion: "Blessed be the name of the LORD from this time forth and for evermore" (Ps. 113:2 KJV).

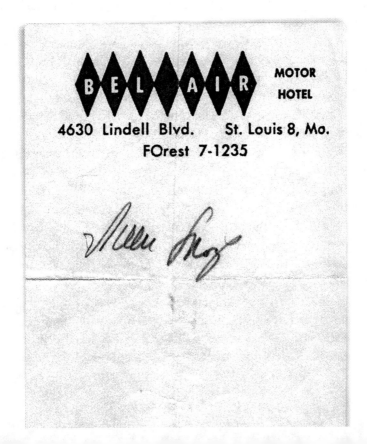

Chastening of the Lord:
A Review of "The Gifts of the Child Christ"

What is your favorite Christmas story?

One of my favorites is "The Gifts of the Child Christ" by George MacDonald. The plot revolves around five-year old Phosy Greatorex of London, who believes the only way the Lord expresses His love is by "chastening." So the little girl thinks "for the hundredth time . . . if the Lord would but chasten me!"

Indeed, it is scriptural that the Lord chastens—corrects, disciplines, instructs, punishes, reproves, scourges—those He loves (Deut. 8:5). Sometimes, God corrects us because we are out of His will. "Stern discipline awaits him who leaves the path; he who hates correction will die" (Prov. 15:10 NIV; see also Ps. 118:18). And in Psalm 119, we find: "Before I was afflicted I went astray, but now I keep Your Word" (Ps. 119:67).

Would you not agree that this "correcting process" is comparable to being placed in the belly of a fish?

The Word also tells us tests and trials are common to all, regardless of the state of our walk with Christ (Matt. 5:45; Rom. 8:18; James 1:2-3). And our sacred text tells us suffering for righteousness' sake is a reality (Matt. 5:11-12; Acts 5:41; 2 Cor. 4:8-9; 2 Tim. 3:12; 1 Pet. 3:14).

Regardless of our sovereign God's reasoning as to why we are going through whatever it is we're going through—that might not be to our liking—it is a fact: the Lord's chastening is for our ultimate good.

"Blessed is the man you discipline, O LORD, the man you teach from your law" (Ps. 94:12 NIV; see also Ps. 94:10; 1 Cor. 11:32; Heb. 12:5-6; 1 Pet. 4:17; Rev. 3:19).

In addition to Phosy Greatorex' ongoing, wishful thinking—that the Lord would chasten her to show His love toward her—she faces difficult circumstances at home: Phosy's mother is dead; and her dad and step-mom are preoccupied with other things (Matt. 13:19-23; Mark 4:19). That is, Mr. and Mrs. Greatorex simply do not see "the hungry heart under the mask of the still face." And by the end of the first chapter, we get the picture: the innocent child is starved for affection. She is caught in the thick of a vast chastening forest, and the good fruit from it—accomplishing "far more abundantly beyond all" that she could ask or think (Eph. 3:20)—has not yet come forth. Furthermore, Phosy's nurse abandons the child "almost entirely to her own resources." So Phosy often sits "alone in the nursery, wishing the Lord would chasten her—because then He would love her."

George MacDonald (1824-1905), a Scottish writer and theologian who greatly influenced the writings of C. S. Lewis (1898-1963), is a master story-teller. In fact, this fifty-seven-year old reader "melted like butter" over Phosy Greatorex as MacDonald thoughtfully weaves the seven-chapter story around the little girl's "character and preciousness." His sentiment toward the child, in view of her trying circumstances at home, is clear: "It is wonderful out of what spoiled fruit some children will suck sweetness."

Similarly, I was reminded of the scripture: "Out of the mouth of babes and sucklings hast thou ordained strength . . ." (Ps. 8:2 KJV).

While I don't want to give away the ending of "The Gifts of the Child Christ," let me assure you: transformation takes place. Love grows broad and long and high and deep (Eph. 3:17-19), and "the small Christian" Phosy—with her transparent expressions of love in a heightened time of confusion and grief—changes the household from "a sunless atmosphere" to "the first of a new covenant."

Chastening brings forth communion. Communion brings forth change. God's people decrease, and God increases (John 3:30). Like the walls at Jericho (Josh. 6:20), the walls of pride at No. 1 Wimborne Square, tumble down. That is, an immature love among the adults gives way to a greater love.

No doubt, the catalyst for change is five-year old Phosy Greatorex, who "was never out of the region of wonders, and would have believed, or tried to believe, anything that did not involve a moral impossibility." Even Phosy's small, but honest, understanding of God's love—including her mistaken, but tender, belief that "the baby Jesus was [literally] born every Christmas Day afresh"—sets into motion the power of God's love toward the entire cast of characters.

In chapter 1 of "The Gifts of the Child Christ," we learn that Phosy's real name is "Sophy," and "by a transposition of consonant sounds common with children," she calls herself "Phosy." That calls to mind another transposition truth: While the Lord chastens those He loves, He loves those He chastens—for "God is love" (1 John 4:8b). That is, our gracious God does not chasten and then love; He loves and then chastens.

Whether God's discipline is mild or sharp, self-directed or group-directed, limited in time or stretched over time, its purpose is for our ultimate good: to bring us to conformity to the image of Jesus Christ (Rom. 8:28-29).

What an awesome gift that is: from the Christ Child to the child Christ within us.

". . . Christ in you, the hope of glory" (Col. 1:27).

[Note: "The Gifts of the Child Christ" can be found online, including this site: *http://tcpiii.tripod.com/childchrist.htm.*]

Daylight Saving Time

Did you realize God actually changed time on a couple occasions? His own version of "fall back" to Standard Time, as compared to "spring forward" to Daylight Saving Time. In one instance, God stopped the sun for approximately a day, and in another God moved the position of the sun.

In Joshua 10, the enemy surrounded Joshua and if darkness fell, the Amorites would overpower him and his army. So, Joshua prayed that the sun "stand still at Gibeon" and the "moon in the valley of Aijalon." Unbelievably, "the sun stood still, and the moon stopped, until the nation avenged themselves of their enemies." Right there "in the middle of the sky," the sun stopped. And it "did not hasten to go down for about a whole day" (Josh. 10:12-13).

As if to re-emphasize His "I-can-change-time" abilities, God does it again. In 2 Kings, chapter 20, we read that King Hezekiah was very sick and the prophet Isaiah visited him, telling Hezekiah that he was not going to die. In fact, the LORD was going to add fifteen years to Hezekiah's life (Isa. 38:5). In his doubt and cynicism, Hezekiah expects a sign of proof from Isaiah (2 Kings 20:8)—and he got it: the sun miraculously went backwards ten degrees as visually demonstrated by a shadow on a stairway moving back ten steps (2 Kings 20:9-11; Isa. 38:5-8). Our God of all creation controls time—miraculously on at least these two occasions.

Furthermore, we can find spiritual implications in the phrase, "Daylight Saving Time." Each word reminds me of aspects of God's attributes and promises.

Linda L. Scisson
P.O. Box 23868
Little Rock, AR 72221-3868

lindascisson@sbcglobal.net

(501) 225-3513
Cell Ph. 412-2024

601 Napa Valley Dr., #423

DAYLIGHT

Day and light are metaphors for God, either as the Father, the Son, or the Holy Spirit. In the Old Testament, we're told that light dwells with God (Dan. 2:22 NIV). And this concept is expanded in the New Testament: "God is light, and in him is no darkness at all" (1 John 1:5 KJV). "I have come into the world as light, so that everyone who believes in me should not remain in the darkness" (John 12:46 GNT). And, Jesus calls His followers "The light of the world—like a city on a mountain, glowing in the night for all to see" (Matt. 5:14 NLT).

SAVING

God, through His Son Jesus Christ, is in the business of saving. Jesus clearly speaks of salvation. "For I did not come to judge the world, but to save the world" (John 12:47). The Word also says, "For whosoever shall call upon the name of the Lord shall be saved" (Rom. 10:13 KJV). Salvation is found in no one else (Acts 4:12 NIV).

TIME

Among several time references, we find these in the Bible: "for a long time now" (2 Chron. 15:3); "God's time finally came—how God tested his patience" (Ps. 105:19); and "a time of great and joyful celebration" (Neh. 8:12). Also, God lets us know His thoughts on time in Ecclesiastes: "Everything is appropriate in its own time" (Eccles. 3:11). Or, as chapter 3 begins, "There is a right time for everything" (Eccles. 3:1 TLB). We should ask the Author of time and space to "teach us to make the most of our time, so that we may grow in wisdom" (Ps. 90:12 NLT).

Each fall season, when Daylight Saving Time ends and we fall back to Standard Time, we see the days become shorter, the nights longer, the air cooler. Birds migrate, animals hibernate, and the landscape changes by our God who "changes times and seasons" (Dan. 2:21 NIV). As we see the changes around us, may we be reminded that our timeless God is sovereign over all creation and we can "fall back" on Him.

13
Downsizing

If you have ever tried to downsize, as I have, a tape measure is a practical tool. It helps me determine what will fit into this new, compact-size residence. Not only do I need to measure the length, but also the width of each room and each piece of furniture. For instance, maybe I can place my huge, old desk against one wall in the small study, but will I be able to put a chair in front of the desk and still be able to move around? Knowing the dimensions of the room and the furniture will let me know what will fit.

God is interested in measurements, too. When God told Moses to build the tabernacle, He gave specific instructions concerning measurements of the tabernacle and the courtyard. A certain pattern was to be followed. A study of the Tabernacle helps us understand the steps God provided for a sinful people to approach a holy God. For example, the Tabernacle was to be placed in the center of the camp, to signify its prime importance in the lives of the people. Details on the tabernacle are found in the book of Exodus, chapters 25-27.

God saw the advantage of downsizing, too, as reflected in His conversation with Gideon in Judges 7:2. Less is more in God's eyes—at least on this occasion: "And the LORD said to Gideon, 'The people who are with you are too many for Me to give Midian into their hands, lest Israel become boastful, saying, 'My own power has delivered me'" (Judg. 7:2). So, God instructed Gideon to downsize the troops from 32,000 (Judg. 7:3) to, well, guess how many? A cut of 50 percent would have left an army of 16,000. A cut of 75 percent would have rejected 24,000 soldiers, leaving only 8,000. What did God do? He kicked it down a notch 99.0625 percent—from an army of 32,000 to only 300 (Judg. 7:8).

"'Not by might, nor by power, but by My Spirit,'
says the Lord Almighty" (ZECH. 4:6 NIV).

Downsizing can be looked at from other angles, too. Take the root word, "down." Manna fell down from heaven at the same time the dew fell down on the camp of the Israelites (Num. 11:9). The apostle Paul purposely falls down as he bows his knees before the Father in a posture of prayer (Eph. 3:14). The roots of trees and plants extend down into the ground in order to grow. We dig down into the earth to obtain natural resources. Gravity pulls things down and gives objects their weight, just as God's Word extends deep into the ground of our souls—giving us identity, affirmation, and truth (Isa. 61:11).

My earthly father, Keathley Scisson (1919-1996), had a unique way of disciplining my twin sister and me. When we got too rowdy, Dad would look at us more stern than usual and say, "Down, sisters." That's all he would say. That's all he had to say. And when we sisters "downsized" our misbehavior, we returned to Daddy's good graces.

Does not our heavenly Father want us to go down in order to get up? He calls us to get off our high horse of pride and go down into the fertile ground of humility. Because that's where He lifts us to a higher plane, where the fruit of His Holy Spirit (Gal. 5:22-23) can grow. "Humble yourselves in the sight of the Lord, and He shall lift you up" (James 4:10 KJV). Or, how about this twin verse: "He [Jesus Christ] must increase, but I must decrease" (John 3:30).

Jesus hung His head down when He was crucified. Being nailed to the cross, Jesus could no longer hold his head up. Considering the crown of thorns on His head (Mark 15:17), it is reasonably certain that Jesus' blood dropped right in front of the cross, which is foreshadowed in the Old Testament. At the Tabernacle on the Day of Atonement, the priest was commanded to sprinkle blood from the sacrificed animal directly in front of the mercy seat (Lev. 16:14). At the crucifixion, we see the blood sprinkled downward from the head of Jesus—acting as our great High Priest (Heb. 9:11)—right in front of the cross, as a symbol of God's mercy for us through the sacrificial death of His Son, Jesus Christ.

> "Behold, the Lamb of God who takes away the sin of the world!" (JOHN 1:29).

There is no tape measure that can measure the love of Jesus Christ. A 12-foot tape measure is too small. Ditto with a 16-footer, a 25-footer, or even the contractor-size, 100-foot tape measure. But we are told that Paul, a former persecutor of Christians (Acts 9:1), has prayed that we will be ". . . rooted and grounded in love" and "able to comprehend with all the saints what is the breadth and length and height and depth" of the love of Jesus Christ (Eph. 3:17-18). *That* covers a lot of square footage. That passage is packed with cosmic dimensions. Better yet, God promises that He is able to "carry out His purpose" and do "infinitely beyond our highest prayers, desires, thoughts, hopes or dreams" (Eph. 3:20 AMP).

How wide is God's love? How long is God's love? How high and how deep is it? I do not know. But God wants me to know the love of Jesus Christ "that surpasses knowledge" and to "be filled to the measure of all the fullness of God" (Eph. 3:19 NIV). God indeed wants me to fit into His love. God's holy floor plan has a place for me. There's plenty of room. In fact, the Word says He does not want anyone to be left out: "Not wishing for any to perish but for all to come to repentance" (2 Pet. 3:9).

That reminds me of several years ago, when I felt extremely anxious in social settings. One evening at the height of my anxiety, having returned home from a social function, I leaned over the kitchen sink and cried out, "Oh God, I don't fit in with this group. I don't fit in with that group. I don't fit in anywhere." In one of those unexpected moments of clearly hearing God's voice in my spirit, God thundered back: "FIT IN WITH ME" (John 15:4).

14

Dressage

We can compare our ability to respond to God's barely perceptible signals to dressage: "the execution by a trained horse of precision movements in response to barely perceptible signals from its rider" (*Merriam-Webster's Collegiate Dictionary*). These "barely perceptible signals" are like God's whispers, requiring experienced ears to hear. As C. S. Lewis wrote in *The Problem of Pain*, "God whispers to us in our pleasures, speaks in our conscience, but shouts in our pain: it is His megaphone to rouse a deaf world."

I imagine many of us have experienced these three signals at one time or another. God has *whispered*, God has *spoken*, and God has *shouted*. I prefer His whispers and His "normal" tone of voice. He shouts when I'm most hard-headed, as I have found truth in the Scriptures: "The LORD disciplines those He loves" (Prov. 3:12 NIV), as His "correction is always right and for our best . . ." (Heb. 12:10 TLB).

Beth Moore once said if we don't voluntarily fall on our knees, God will break us at the knees. I compare that to God's shouts, which remind me of one of the final scenes in the movie "The Horse Whisperer" where the trainer *makes* the horse, Pilgrim, fall to the ground. He hobbles the horse's front left foot and lays him down in the dust and dirt (Isa. 25:12).

In this grounded position, the humbled horse is finally ready to be re-introduced to his beloved rider, a girl whose first name is Grace. After experiencing a horrible accident, both horse and rider needed affirmation upon affirmation before they could be linked back together. Pilgrim, the horse, especially needed a sense of being able to trust again. And like our wise God, the trainer knew beforehand the favorable outcome of "humbling" Pilgrim at this point in the healing process. (And aren't we all on a spiritual pilgrimage?)

In other words, God does not "break us" for the mere sake of "breaking us;" God breaks us to make us more like His image (Hosea 6:1).

When we obey God's whispers and His "normal" tone of voice, we can avoid being lassoed by God, thrown to the ground, and caught up in all the dust and dirt. Obedience makes it possible to avoid unnecessary future pain, not only upon ourselves, but upon others, as well. When God corrects us, He does not want to embarrass us. The Holy Spirit is a gentle spirit. "A battered reed He will not break off . . ." (Matt. 12:20). And Matthew 1:19 reads, "Because Mary's husband, Joseph, was a good man, he did not want to disgrace her in public . . ." (Matt. 1:19 NCV). Likewise, God, being a good God, does not want to disgrace us. But I have found that He will lasso me to the ground, even with a crowd watching over the corral fence, if He has to resort to that drastic of a measure to get me to see things His way.

I believe that's why God, speaking through His Son, Jesus, gives us a pattern to follow in sticky situations:

> "If another believer sins against you, go privately and point out the fault. If the other person listens and confesses it, you have won that person back. But if you are unsuccessful, take one or two others with you and go back again, so that everything you say may be confirmed by two or three witnesses. If that person still refuses to listen, take your case to the church. If the church decides you are right, but the other person won't accept it, treat that person as a pagan or a corrupt tax collector"
> (MATT. 18:15-17 NLT).

These are definite stages—one, two, and three—with each step up the ladder being more serious. *The first stage*—one to one (Matt. 18:15): I compare that to God speaking above a whisper . . . in a soft, reasonable voice, hoping to get my attention here. But if I don't "take heed," He moves me to *the second stage*—bringing in one or two others on the scene (Matt. 18:16): I compare that to God's "speaking to our con-science" on a deeper level. And, if absolutely necessary, God takes me to *the third stage*—where the church is involved (Matt. 18:17): That's like "God shouting in His megaphone." But His absolute grace is there, too, at this critical juncture. Our God who begs us to turn our laughter into mourning over our sins (James 4:9) is the same God who says He "will wipe away the tears from all faces" (Isa. 25:8 NIV). Talk about a balance of God's justice and His mercy. Wow.

In *Dressage: Harmony between Horse and Rider*, Gary Lashinsky, the producer of Lipizzaner Stallions World Tour, describes dressage as "the art of perfecting the natural gait. It is the perfect walk, the precise trot, and the even cantor."

Dressage is French for "training." It is harmony between horse and rider: a state comparable to an experienced Christian, a mature fol-lower of Jesus Christ, walking with "hope and faith" that are "strong and steady;" and moving along with "heads high," as God's "warm love" is clearly known and dearly felt (Rom. 5:4-5 TLB). Here God resorts to "barely perceptible signals." Here "God whispers to us in our pleasures." Here is harmony between creation and Creator.

I find it most inspiring to see a brother or sister in Christ in this "arena." To see this depth of spiritual maturity makes me want to have it myself. And times when God has whispered to me and I've rightly responded to His "barely perceptible signals," it's nice. It's very nice. It's where I finally get it: that yes, "*His* yoke is easy" (Matt. 11:30 KJV, emphasis added). And yes, "His Truth *makes* me free" (John 8:32 KJV, emphasis added).

As we seek God's grace, may we respond appropriately to His truth, whether it comes to us as "barely perceptible signals" as in a whisper; in a natural tone of voice (as in our routine reading of God's Word); or as a megaphone shout (as in times of pain or continuous disobedience). And may we allow ourselves to be trained by God—the Father, Son, and Holy Spirit—and subsequently execute, like a highly trained horse, "the perfect walk, the precise trot, and the even cantor," enabling us to "excel still more" (1 Thess. 4:1).

15

Facials

Have you had a facial lately? A spiritual facial, where God restores the glow to your face and your soul—inspiring the Psalmist to write: "Your face, O LORD, I shall seek" (Ps. 27:8)?

Whereas a facial at a spa takes about an hour, there are "facials" in the Old Testament that lasted an entire year. Women participated in beauty treatments that lasted twelve months, which included "six months with oil of myrrh, followed by six months with special perfumes and ointments" (Esther 2:12 NLT).

What is the significance of this Old Testament custom for us today?

In the course of sanctification, one could say God gives His daughters and sons two types of facials or beauty treatments: (1) a relaxing facial with a massage, moisturizer, and mist—where we bask in His presence, soaking up all the attention God lavishes on us, and (2) a deep pore-cleansing facial with exfoliation and extraction that is more advanced in its techniques, even a bit painful at times.

These two types of beauty treatments from our God come in seasons.

THE FIRST SEASON

We count the cost of the expensive "oil of myrrh" (Esther 2:12 NLT), and we choose to accept Jesus Christ as our Savior and Lord, along with the anointed call on our lives (Ps. 45:7). As new creations in Christ (2 Cor. 5:17), though zestful in our new-found faith, we drink only milk, rather than solid food (1 Cor. 3:2). Yet, we are prompted by the

Holy Spirit—and encouraged by His Church—to grow in grace, knowledge, and good works (2 Pet. 3:18; Eph. 2:10), as Jesus himself increased in wisdom (Luke 2:52).

THE SECOND SEASON

After our initial growth in the first season, a new season begins, marked by purification: a thorough washing and cleansing of our innermost being (Dan. 12:10; Eph. 5:26-27). God calls us to examine not only the profound things, but the hidden things (Dan. 2:22; Matt. 23:25-26). He tells us to renew our minds (Rom. 12:2; Phil. 4:8). Unexpected trials arise, as God tests our faith (Isa. 48:10; James 1:2-4, 12). He purifies and perfects—comparable to a deep, pore-cleansing facial with exfoliation and extraction.

In the course of all this, somewhat surprisingly (with all the tests and trials), we are drawn into a deeper intimacy. The holy call on our lives birthed in the first season, blooms in the second (Heb. 5:13-14). We find a deeper love for God and a deeper desire to obey Him (Heb. 5:8). As we enter into intimacy with God—by way of humility, prayer, seeking His face, and turning from our wicked ways (2 Chron. 7:14)—we begin to exhibit a certain glow. God bathes us "with special perfumes and ointments" (Esther 2:12 NLT), enabling us to spread the fragrance of Jesus Christ (2 Cor. 2:14-16).

Here, one could say: we become beautiful (Ps.45:11).

Here, one could see how the prophet Isaiah could say: "For your husband is your Maker, whose name is the LORD of hosts . . ." (Isa. 54:5; Hosea 2:19-20).

Like King Xerxes chose Esther to be his queen (Esther 2:17) after she took part in the prescribed, lengthy beauty treatments (Esther 2:12), our King of Kings imparts His beauty—His glow, His grace—on those individuals who consistently and tenaciously draw near unto Him (James 4:8). But if we get into pride and "walk with heads held high and seductive eyes" (Isa. 3:16), our appearance will be affected in a negative fashion. In fact, we are subject to having beauty stripped from us (Isa. 3:16-24; see also Hosea 6:1).

In September 2002, a strange bump on my chin led me to a dermatology clinic. Fortunately, it was benign. The microscopic exam revealed

"an ulcerated vascular lesion . . . consistent with a pyogenic granuloma."
One website gave a parenthetical definition for "pyogenic granuloma"
as being "proud flesh." When I saw those two words, "proud flesh," I
cringed. It was like being catapulted out of denial and into reality—concerning pride in several areas of my life, which I confessed as sin, as I
held on to the Lord's promise that upon confession "He is faithful and
just to forgive us our sins and to cleanse us from all unrighteousness"
(1 John 1:9 NKJV).

In *Mere Christianity*, C. S. Lewis writes that pride is "a terrible
thing;" "spiritual cancer;" "the essential vice, the utmost evil;" "the
complete anti-God state of mind."

Having my "proud flesh" cleansed and cauterized by a dermatologist—and waiting for the wound to heal—is not as fun as having my face
massaged, moisturized, and wrapped in a hot towel by an aesthetician.
I'm reminded of a line in *Shadowlands* where C. S. "Jack" Lewis says: "we
are like blocks of stone that God, like a sculptor, carves and allows the
blows of His chisel to hurt us so much in order to make us perfect."

The lyrics of Barbra Streisand's "That Face" remind me of the face
of Jesus this hour in heaven: "that wonderful face" that "shines" and
"glows all over the place," that's "in a class beyond compare." Indeed,
the face of Jesus is "like the sun shining in all its brilliance" (Rev. 1:16
NIV). And a life seeking our Lord's face draws us into a love for Him
that shows as a glow on our faces and our souls (Dan. 12:3; Ps. 80:3; 2
Cor. 3:16-18).

> "The LORD bless you and keep you;
> The LORD make His face shine upon you,
> and be gracious to you;
> The LORD lift up His countenance upon you,
> and give you peace"
> (NUM. 6:24-26 NKJV).

Geography 101

Geography 101 would tell us that mountains are high places and valleys low places. Isn't this also true, metaphorically, in Bible 101?

Take the phrase: "though I walk through the shadow of the valley of death" (Ps. 23:4). Obviously, "the valley of death" represents a low point in one's life. But the good news: The valley is only a "shadow" with the promise that we can walk through it.

With regard to high places, one mountain that represents an elevated sense of inspiration is Mount Carmel. On the top of Mount Carmel, the prophet Elijah prayed for rain to end a severe drought (1 Kings 18:2, 42-45). Did he get what he prayed for? Yes. "There was a heavy shower" (1 Kings 18:45; James 5:17-18).

Before Elijah climbed to the top of Mount Carmel, he took part in a contest on a plateau halfway up the mountain. At this plateau, God revealed His supernatural powers by way of a literal consuming fire, commanded by the prophet Elijah (1 Kings 18:24). This divine intervention was a huge victory for Elijah and the God he serves: *Yahweh*: The "I AM"; the LORD who is faithful, who never changes, whose promises never fail. And it was a huge loss, eventually leading to death, for Elijah's contenders: the false prophets of false gods who had "forsaken the commandments of the LORD" to follow the Baals and the Asherah (1 Kings 18:17-19).

Would you agree that most of life's contests—the "fiery" trials (1 Pet. 4:12 KJV)—are not on the mountain top or in the valley? Most of life's contests are on the plateau. Perhaps this is where the character quality, perseverance, meets its match. We will probably turn to God when we're in a valley. We will probably praise Him from the mountain top. But on a plateau? At mid-point in our journey with new and unexpected trials? At halftime in the game of life with little change in a trying circumstance? At a place where there is no drought, no devastating flood, but the sound of distant thunder that upsets our picnic with perseverance. On such a plateau, do we still offer God Most High (*El Elyon*) a "sacrifice of praise"? (Heb. 13:15-16).

What is it that causes Jan Karon, author of the Mitford Series, to make a statement like this? "A miracle! Let no one ever say or even think that God does not work miracles, still; every common day, every common life is filled with them. . . ." Has she tasted the abundant life? Has she glimpsed the Shekinah glory? Has she grown in grace? Has she hoisted herself onto the highway of holiness (Isa. 35:8-10 NIV)? Has she purposed in her heart to walk in joy? "This is the day which the LORD has made; let us rejoice and be glad in it" (Ps. 118:24).

Our sacred text speaks of perseverance. In addition to the second and third chapters of Revelation, the Holy Spirit often brings to my remembrance this simple statement: "Let us not lose heart in doing good, for in due time we will reap if we do not grow weary" (Gal. 6:9). On a similar note, Hebrews tells us, "Do not neglect doing good and sharing, for with such sacrifices God is pleased" (Heb. 13:16).

Let's pretend we were asked to give a community a biblical name. Whether the place is in the city or the country, what name would you like to add to the map? My first choice would be "Prayer," because I think perseverance is related to prayer. In fact, I would like to meet some folks who could say without a hint of self-righteousness (Matt. 6:5), "We're from Prayer, and we persevere in prayer." On second thought, I bet that statement is a sweet reality. I bet a random survey would show prayer across the United States of America:

There's prayer in Phoenix & Paducah.
There's prayer in Pinetown & Pine Haven.
Peachtree City & Ponca City, Pearl City & Pell City.
There's prayer in Piney Green & Pioneer.

There's prayer in Pine Bluff & Poplar Bluff.
There's prayer in Pleasant Point & Pleasant View.
Pablo & Palo, Pecos & Pasco.
There's prayer in Platte & Point Hope.

There's prayer in Plano & Polo.
There's prayer in Paragon & Paradise.
Page & Parchment, Pigeon & Parachute.
There's prayer in Paramount & Perkins Corner.

There's prayer in Pittsburgh & Pearisburg.
There's prayer in Petal & Proctor.
Port Charlotte & Port Chester, Portsmouth & Portland.
There's prayer in Parsons & Priest River.

There's prayer in Palisades Park & Park Rapids.
There's prayer in Phillips & Philippi.
Peru & Parole, Promontory & Prosperity.
There's prayer in Provincetown & Providence.

There's prayer in the inner room (Matt. 6:6),
There's prayer in the upper room (Acts 1:13-14).
In many a city, town & village,
There's prayer throughout the USA.

As followers of Jesus Christ, let's persevere on the pinnacle, the plateau, and the valley. Let's persevere in the shadow lands and the high lands. Let's persevere through the fiery trials with a sacrifice of praise. Let's persevere through the major, minor, and mediocre. Let's persevere through the bleak landscape and the lush. Let's persevere on a prayer path to our promised land (Heb. 11:16).

As I believe our God Most High, who never changes, whose promises are true, must like the ring of that: "I'm from Prayer, Arkansas, United States of America . . . and I persevere in prayer."

"Even those I [the LORD] will bring to My holy mountain
And make them joyful in My house of prayer.
Their burnt offerings and their sacrifices will be acceptable on
My altar;
For My house will be called a house of prayer for all the peo-
ples"
(ISA. 56:7).

God's Carvings:
A review of Beyond The Gates of Splendor

"Every family has a story. How my family became part of a stone-age Amazon tribe is a story that began before I was born. . . ." That is the opening narration in *Beyond the Gates of Splendor*, a 96-minute documentary about five USA missionary families that go to Ecuador in the 1950s to connect with an isolated tribe, the Aucas, now known as the Waodani. While all five men are killed in 1956, I couldn't help but think, at the film's conclusion, that "God causes all things to work together for good to those who love God, to those who are called according to His purpose" (Rom. 8:28).

The narrator is Steve Saint, son of Nate Saint, the pilot of the mission. At the start, Steve gives us a look at the geography around the Amazon River and Andes Mountains with its rainforest far below, as well as its people. For instance, the Quechuas, an Indian tribe of Ecuador, refer to another tribe, located deep in the rainforests of eastern Ecuador, as "Aucas," which means "naked savage." In other words, these nomads of the rainforest "held the twentieth century at bay with nothing but . . . spears."

Before telling the story from the perspective of the surviving missionaries' wives and other family members and friends, anthropologists Clayton and Carole Robarchek offer insight, based on researching five generations of the Waodani tribe. Also, interviews are shared with seven members of the Waodani.

Historically speaking, a Waodani child grew up with the understanding that they would "spear and live or be speared and die." Clayton Robarchek adds, "The warring nature of the Waodani reached inside its own groups. Blood feuds and vendettas began an internal cycle of killing on such a huge scale that it threatened the very existence of the tribe."

What struck me with a state close to shock was the casualness of the descriptions of the killings by surviving tribe members. The Waodani interviewed spoke of their relatives being speared in what appears to be normal, conversational tones. Their focus was what part of the body the victim was speared. For example, Kimo says, "Itaeca speared my mother here and here (as he gestures on his own body). Moipa speared her back."

Yet, after a remarkable transformation, Mincaye, one of the warring tribesmen, remarks in hindsight: "We acted badly, badly, until [the missionaries] brought us 'God's Carvings.' Now we walk His trail." Also, I noted on the credits at the end of the movie a special thanks to "The God Followers of the Waodani for their love and hospitality to the Kowodi [outsiders]."

What caused the transformation? What broke the cycle of violence, where previously "six out of every ten Waodani deaths for the past five generations were homicide"? The answer? Knowledge, which reminds me of two scriptures:

"My people are destroyed for lack of knowledge"
(HOSEA 4:6).

". . . you will *know* the truth, and the truth will make you free"
(JOHN 8:32, EMPHASIS ADDED).

Before receiving and assimilating knowledge, primarily from Elisabeth Elliot (wife of murdered Jim Elliot), Rachel Saint (sister of murdered Nate Saint), and Steve Saint (narrator and son of Nate Saint), the Waodani knew of no healthy way to solve conflict. Violence followed after any "violation of the way things ought to be." That is, if someone made you angry, you speared them. In Carole Robarchek's words, the Waodani had "no method, no institutionalized method for resolving conflict." Her husband Clayton adds, "And given that, there is no over-arching mechanism for controlling people's behavior. People simply are able to do precisely what they please." The result of this anger turned into something worse than rage. "An endless litany: virtually everyone's ancestors were speared to death."

Clayton Robarchek's summary of the social relations of the Waodani before becoming aware of a healthier way of living:

> There is no precedent in Waodani culture for submerging your
> own self-interest in the service of a larger group. That idea just
> hasn't existed in the past, so people are unwilling to concede
> any of their freedom of action in service of the objectives of the
> group as a whole, because the group as a whole never existed
> before.

Against such broad strokes of insight into the Waodani, the movie turns: We hear from family members of the slain missionaries. We see their courage and their grief. We see the carvings of God's grace on the faces and in the voices of Elisabeth, the widow of Jim Elliot; Olive, the widow of Pete Fleming; Marilou, the widow of Ed McCully; Marj, widow of Nate Saint; and Barbara, the widow of Roger Youderian. Their love for their husbands is obvious, as they reminisce when they became engaged, as well as share light-hearted incidents, particularly while they were in college.

To accent the power of forgiveness and reconciliation, the documentary lets us hear from other family members, including Jim and Elisabeth Elliot's daughter, Valerie; Nate and Marj Saint's daughter, Kathy; and grandsons, Jesse Saint and Jaime Saint (i.e., the narrator's sons). Before the documentary's end, other names become familiar: Mincaye, Ompodae, Nenkiwi ("George"), Gimade ("Delilah"), Dayumae, Kimo, and Tementa.

Beyond the Gates of Splendor speaks of "missionaries trying to bring them the Word of God—to tell them about a different reality." After a history of one senseless tragedy after another, circumstances changed. God's redemptive love becomes imparted to the Waodani. As Clayton Robarchek remarks:

It was only when new information became available to them that they could see that there were, in fact, other possibilities. Rachel [Saint] and Elisabeth [Elliot] wanted people to believe that there was a God who wanted them to stop killing.

"The Waodani were able in just a few years to reduce the homicide rate by well over 90 per cent.

"What changed was the information people had available to them. And on the basis of that, they made a radical transformation in their social life."

Why would one venture deep into such places? One must be called. One must sense God's leading to go and "make disciples of all the nations, baptizing them in the name of the Father and the Son and the Holy Spirit", and "teaching them to observe all" that Jesus has commanded (Matt. 28:19-20).

God's Golden Gift

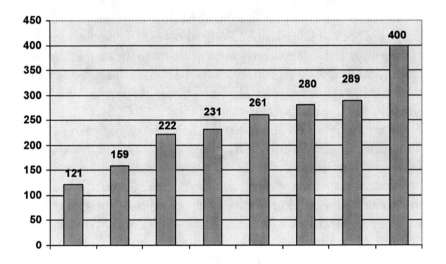

What word appears more times in the Bible than faith? More times than hope? More times than love? Answer: Peace. When I researched several words related to Christianity, here's the number of times each word appears in the King James Version.

Peace   400
Righteousness   289
Love   280
Mercy   261

Faith	231
Truth	222
Wisdom	222
Grace	159
Hope	121

With peace topping the list, God must know we need a generous supply. The good news: With the golden shovel of the Bible, not only can we break up fallow ground (Jer. 4:3; Hosea 10:12 KJV) and gather knowledge about peace, we can experience it. After all, commentator Matthew Henry writes (in reference to Genesis 2:9, 16-17 and Proverbs 13:12), "The tree of life is better than the tree of knowledge."

Let's dig up a few of the four hundred sites on peace:

In the book of John, Jesus' parting words to His disciples included a going away gift. What do you suppose that was? Peace via the Holy Spirit (John 14:26). Jesus said, "I am leaving you with a gift—peace of mind and heart! And the peace I give isn't fragile like the peace the world gives. So don't be troubled or afraid" (John 14:27 TLB).

In the Hebrew Old Testament, peace is *shalom*, in the Greek New Testament, *eirene*. Spiros Zodhiates, in *The Complete Word Study Dictionary, New Testament*, defines *eirene* as "a sense of divine favor," "wholeness, soundness, hence health, well-being, prosperity . . . the absence of confusion." Furthermore, biblical peace is "tranquility, arising from reconciliation with God," "a blessing of which God alone is the author," "a gift which God desires to impart to all His people, but which He is often unable to grant because of their sins."

In two words, what is one way to know God's will? Follow peace (Phil. 4:9; Heb. 12:14). If I do not have peace—which I realize the enemy of my soul fights to steal (John 10:10)—it's usually a red-flag in my spirit that I'm out of the will of God. That is, anxiety is often linked with being alienated or estranged from God. Like the word "strange" appears in "estranged," I feel strange and I'm often acting strange (or out of character) when I'm not following God in some aspect of my life. Yet, if I have peace, I'm more than likely in my heavenly Father's will, in His favor; and out of the grip of *sin*, a word which appears 389 times in the Bible. The word *holy* appears an off-the-chart 544 times.

To help us know God's best in a situation, we can pray: "Lord, if You have put this decision, idea, or thought in my heart, may I experience Your peace. And show me, without any doubt, what Your peace is." What happens next? On some level, "the peace of God, which surpasses all understanding" is sent our way. That's how the apostle Paul describes it. And it's a peace that "will guard your hearts and minds through Christ Jesus" (Phil. 4:7 NKJV).

Prayer cannot be over-emphasized in our quest for God's peace. In this same letter to the Philippians, but in another translation, we're given more insight:

> Don't fret or worry. Instead of worrying, pray. Let petitions
> and praises shape your worries into prayers, letting God know
> your concerns. Before you know it, a sense of God's wholeness,
> everything coming together for good, will come and settle you
> down. It's wonderful what happens when Christ displaces
> worry at the center of your life.
> (PHIL. 4:6-7 MSG; SEE ALSO 1 TIM. 2:1-2).

Needless to say, peace is prominent in the eyes of God. In fact, God is peace (Num. 6:26; Judg. 6:23-24), and so is Jesus (Isa. 9:6; Eph. 2:14). And Jesus preached peace in the Sermon on the Mount. "God blesses those who work for peace, for they will be called the children of God" (Matt. 5:9 NLT). For added understanding, *The Message* reads: "You're blessed when you can show people how to cooperate instead of compete or fight. That's when you discover who you really are, and your place in God's family" (Matt. 5:9 MSG).

The poet tells us: "Righteousness and peace have kissed each other" (Ps. 85:10 KJV). The prophet tells us: "the work of righteousness will be peace . . . " (Isa. 32:17). God tells us, "He will speak peace to His people and to His saints . . . " (Ps. 85:8 NKJV). And may I chime in? We will know God's peace when we experience God's peace. It's not a rise in one's serotonin level. It's not a mere lessening of negative emotions. It's not a shallow blessing to saints and sinners alike (Jer. 8:11). It's something more. It's something better. The peace of God is a precious fruit of the Holy Spirit (Gal. 5:22; see also Rom. 14:11; Heb. 12:11). It is miracle and mystery and movement. God's peace brings supernatural serenity to one's soul (Ps. 25:12-13; Rom. 2:9-10). It's where "we live and move and have our being" (Acts 17:28 KJV). It's where we dwell "in the secret place of the Most High" (Ps. 91:1 KJV). It's where we move out of the bondage of sin and into the blessings of righteousness. God's peace envelops the righteous. God's peace surpasses all comprehension (Phil. 4:7).

Whether I am to "follow peace," "go in peace," "hold my peace," "live in peace," "make peace," or "seek peace," (Heb. 12:14; Acts 16:36; Neh. 8:11; 2 Cor. 13:11; James 3:18; 1 Pet. 3:11 KJV) I am persuaded that God's peace is a worthy pursuit, a holy privilege, a golden gift from Jehovah-shalom (Judg. 6:24 KJV).

Grazing on God's Grace
19

A million years before man, they grazed the vast empty plains . . .
They first came to know man as the hunted knows the hunter,
for long before he used horses for his labors, he killed them for
meat. The alliance with man would forever be fragile. For the
fear he'd struck into their hearts was too deep to be dislodged.

Since that neolithic moment when a horse was first hal-
tered, there were those among men who understood this. They
could see into the creature's soul and soothe the wounds they
found there. The secrets uttered softly into troubled ears, these
men were known as the Whisperers.

THE HORSE WHISPERER
SCREENPLAY BY ERIC ROTH AND RICHARD LAGRAVENESE

Long before sin, man and woman grazed in a beautiful garden—with
no shame, no guilt, no fear. Upon falling into sin, wounded souls came
to see the opposite sex as the hunted knows the hunter. With the advent
of sin, man and woman sometimes used each other and abused each
other. The alliance between them appeared to be forever fragile, as the
fear these instances of misuse and abuse struck deep into their hearts.

Since the Incarnation moment when God became man and dwelt
among us, men and women were introduced to the poverty in their souls
with the strange idea this could be transformed into something better:
an alliance forged on faith, hope, and love. Despite negative coping skills
from the past attempting—and sometimes succeeding—to rear their

heads, a process of transformation began.

By God's grace, He sent men and women who understood these psychological dynamics. They could see into another creature's soul and soothe the wounds they found there. God's truth uttered softly into troubled ears—these men and women were known as the wounded healers.

Out of their wounds came their willingness to persevere. Out of their surrender came their strength. For the wounded healers knew as they shed their own layers of pride, fear, and control—and "let go and let God"—they became God's unbridled instrument not only to help others, but to help themselves.

For in the vast empty places of the wounded healers, the Word of God struck deep. Fear was dislodged, and faith took over.

Perfect love casts out fear (1 JOHN 4:18).

"A battered reed, He will not break off . . ." (MATT. 12:20).

When I am weak, then I am strong (2 COR. 12:10).

He who began a good work in you will perfect it until the day of Christ Jesus (PHIL. 1:6).

Where there is no guidance, the people fall, but in abundance of counselors there is victory (PROV. 11:14).

Now to Him who is able to do exceeding abundantly beyond all that we ask or think, according to the power that works within us, to Him be the glory in the church and in Christ Jesus to all generations forever and ever. Amen (EPH. 3:20-21).

Howdy Doody Time

The Howdy Doody Show was a popular children's television show in the 1950s. It featured the voice of radio performer and musician "Buffalo Bob" Smith and his trusty sidekick, a twenty-seven inch marionette, Howdy. Each show began with the question, "Say kids, what time is it?"

And the response was: "It's Howdy Doody time!"

"It's Howdy Doody time" to spring a few spiritual questions. Do any of these sound familiar?

- How do I "bear much fruit"? (John 15:8)
- How do I "love one another"? (John 13:34)
- How do I "make disciples of all the nations"? (Matt. 28:19)

In response to my "How do I . . . ?" questions, two passages come to mind. Shortly after Jesus introduced himself to two disciples, they asked Him, "Where do you live?" Jesus responded, "Come and see" (John 1:38-39). Now, Jesus could have given a specific location, but all He said were three simple words, "Come and see" (John 1:39 KJV).

Often it seems the Lord has me "come and see" Luke 1:26-35, where an angel tells Mary that she will give birth to the Son of God. Mary's immediate question is, "How can this be?" (Luke 1:34). While Mary is young in age, she is spiritually mature. She does not ask a "Why" question, such as "Why is this happening to me?" Mary asks a "How" question: "How can this be?" (Luke 1:34).

I believe the angel's response to Mary is God's promise to us—

when we doubt our ability, in the natural realm, to do something that God wants us to do. At Luke 1:35, Gabriel tells Mary:

"The Holy Spirit will come upon you, and
the power of the Most High will overshadow you."

The Holy Spirit, as the third Person of the Trinity or "tri-unity," fulfills different roles, one of which is to endow a believer with special gifts to accomplish something distinct. That is, the Holy Spirit gives a believer whatever is necessary—courage, favor, patience, stamina, time—to do what God wants done. While the Holy Spirit indwells every believer from the moment of salvation (Rom. 8:9-11; 1 Cor. 12:13), "re-fillings" in various forms are available, at God's choosing, throughout one's lifetime (John 14:26; Acts 1:8; 1 Cor. 12:3-6).

According to Spiros Zodiates, "The power of the Most High" (Luke 1:35) refers to "the great power of God, meaning His almighty energy." "Overshadow" means "to shade" or "cast a shadow upon." It is "spoken of a divine power and influence, to overshadow, rest upon."

There is a scene in the 1965 movie *The Sound of Music* where Maria and the von Trapp children stand above a stage and sing with uninhibited joy as they maneuver, with great dexterity, marionettes. Like the person who controls the movements of a marionette and gives it life and breath, the Holy Spirit "controls the strings" and generates the great power of God within a believer. Those believers who yield their lives—their day, their decisions, their every breath, and movement—to the leading of the Holy Spirit become trusty sidekicks to this Source of divine energy.

It's not synthetic energy. It's not performance-driven energy. It's not paint by numbers. That is, it's not artificial, legalistic, or mundane. Nor is it manipulation, intimidation, or exploitation: a fruitless "pulling of strings" by a source that does not have our best interests in mind. God's holy energy is supernaturally driven. It is pure and powerful. It is purposeful. It is sweet. God's Holy Spirit impedes our impulse to sin, stills our carnal thoughts, warms and purifies our soul, and fills our hearts with "righteousness and peace and joy" (Rom. 14:17).

God's Spirit brings life to dry bones (Ezek. 37:4-5).

God's Spirit replaces what is spineless—formless and void, dark and empty—with form and structure, fullness and light. God's Spirit reaches beyond the globe (Gen. 1:1-10). God's Spirit resides within the soul (John 14:16-17; Col. 1:27).

- How do we proclaim this "life and breath" invitation to the nations? (Acts 17:25-26)
- How do we "lengthen our cords" and "stretch out the curtains"? (Isa. 54:2)
- How do we share our freedom in Christ (Gal. 5:1) with no strings attached—"leaping with joy like calves let out to pasture"? (Mal. 4:2 NLT)
- How do we show the love of "Abba! Father!" (Mark 14:36; Rom. 8:15; Gal. 4:6), whose creation "waits eagerly for the revealing" of His sons and daughters? (Rom. 8:19)
- How do we go to a "high and holy place" (Isa. 57:15) where "every devoted thing is most holy unto the LORD"? (Lev. 27:28 KJV)
- How do we say, like Mary, "Behold, the handmaid of the Lord; be it unto me according to thy Word"? (Luke 1:38 KJV)
- How do we "come and see"? (John 1:39 KJV) Is it on bended knee?

PRAYER

Gracious God, may Your Holy Spirit come upon us. May the power of the Most High overshadow us. In the Name of the Father, the Son, and the Holy Spirit. Amen.

In High Fashion

Are you wearing what's in style? Are you in high fashion? I hear there is a wonderful sale on the corner of Heart & Stone (Jer. 31:33; Ezek. 36:26). Look for the clothing store named "Strength & Dignity." Across the street, you'll find the equally popular outlet store, "Righteousness."

It's a trend, an attribute, a character quality of followers of Jesus Christ: We dress alike. To be on God's "Best Dressed List," we put on Strength, Dignity, and Righteousness—regardless of the weather outside, regardless of our feelings inside, regardless of the number of years we've adorned ourselves with "lesser threads" (which goes back to Adam & Eve making aprons out of fig leaves (Gen. 3:7). Clearly, to remain in high fashion—to be in vogue as authentic Christians—we wear the elite "SDR" label. We dress ourselves in Strength, Dignity, and Righteousness.

"Back that up with Scriptures – chapter and verse," you say.

Okay. One of the proverbs reads—in partial description of an excellent wife: "*Strength* and *dignity* are her clothing" (Prov. 31:25a, emphasis added). Since one principle of biblical interpretation from the Reformation is Scripture interprets Scripture, and reading in Galatians 3:28 that we "are all one in Christ Jesus" (whether male or female), I don't believe I strain biblical interpretation by saying strength and dignity apply to all Christians.

Insofar as *righteousness*, the prophet Isaiah writes:

"I will rejoice greatly in the LORD,
My soul will exult in my God;
For He has clothed me with garments of salvation,
He has wrapped me with a robe of *righteousness* . . ."
(ISA. 61:10, EMPHASIS ADDED).

Zechariah unravels more good news: "See, I have taken your iniquity away from you and will clothe you with festal robes" (Zech. 3:4b). That reminds me of the day I put on a choir robe at a local Christian bookstore and looked at myself in the mirror. I wanted to see myself in "a festal robe." I needed a visual. I liked the way I looked in this symbolic "robe of righteousness."

A wise friend, prolific writer, and brother in Christ named Paul encourages us—by way of letters in the New Testament—to dress appropriately. In one letter, Paul writes to "put on the Lord Jesus Christ, and make no provision for the flesh in regard to its lusts" (Rom. 13:14). In another letter, Paul reminds us that "all of you who were baptized into Christ have clothed yourselves with Christ" (Gal. 3:27). In a third letter, our brother instructs us to "put on the full armor of God" and tells us why: "so that you will be able to stand firm against the schemes of the devil" (Eph. 6:11).

Would you agree that these images point toward: Strength, Dignity, and Righteousness?

Since 1949, the winner of the annual Masters Golf Tournament in Augusta, Georgia, has received a green jacket as a victory symbol of having overcome crucial competition, fear on the fairways, grief on the greens, and ridicule in the roughs. Similarly, as "victors in Christ" (1 Cor. 15:57), as "conquerors through Him who loved us" (Rom. 8:37), as "overcomers" of trials and tests throughout our earthly lives (Rev. 2 and 3), one day we will receive a "tournament-winning" white garment (Rev. 3:5, 18). In fact, we will walk with Jesus in white garments (Rev. 3:4). What a walkway that will be.

How's our wardrobe? Everything okay? Need a quick inventory?

Like a short, immodest skirt weakens our witness (1 Tim. 2:9), are we sometimes short with others, which zaps our strength in the Lord? "Be strong in the Lord and in the strength of His might" (Eph. 6:10;

see also Isa. 52:1).

Do we keep our shirt of dignity freshly ironed? That is, do we iron out our differences with dignity and resolve? Or do we allow wrinkles of strife and resentment to "soil our garments" (2 Cor. 12:20; Rev. 3:4)?

Do we think good thoughts about others and ourselves, as we tighten a belt of truth around our waist? Or do our thoughts linger in a dirty-laundry basket (Phil. 4:8; Eph. 6:14; Rom. 1:21; 2 Cor. 10:5)?

Do we wrap ourselves in a robe of righteousness? Are we doing what's loving and right? Or, like Joseph's brothers, are we jealous and hateful over someone else's "coat of many colors" (Gen. 37:3; Deut. 5:21; Prov. 27:4; Acts 5:17; 1 Cor. 13:4; 1 Pet. 5:5)?

God is concerned with the fabric of our lives, each and every thread. He wants to color our lives with good things—His chosen, fine, and royal attributes. He prompts us to stay in high fashion—in His eyes; because "woe is us" when we try to be wise in our own eyes (Isa. 5:21; Gal. 6:7). After all, God is our loving, personal, fashion designer (Ps. 139:13-14; Jer. 1:5). And the word is out: He likes His "supermodels" dressed in Strength, Dignity, and Righteousness.

Maternity Ward

Imagine Jesus is born in a modern-day hospital . . .

A baby is born on Christmas Day
for the world to see through
the window. In a wool blanket
he's snug asleep, pink-faced,
soft, innocent.

Oh God, he touches my heart,
stops the cry of an incubated
sister, severs pain from my soul.
He wiggles his finger for Father,
he delights the gathered throng.

He's the Baby Jesus of the maternity ward
in on the ground floor of crucifixion.

Math Lesson from God

You ask Me to instruct you. I chuckle.
As your Teacher, I find no reason
to reveal more of Me than a fraction.
Your curiosity pleases Me.
Channel it in the right direction.

You hesitate in your walk.
You know the road that adds, you know
the road that subtracts. Believe what I say:
one plus one equals two.

Do not let your mind, nor your flesh
rule over your spirit. Remember
what is eternal. I gave you My Beloved Son,
that includes My Grace. I gave you My Holy Spirit,
that includes My Power. I gave you a glimpse of Me —
that completes the Trinity.

Once again, you say you wait on Me
to move in your life. You long
for a "road to Damascus" experience.
On the contrary, I wait on you,
the Teacher's pet, for one more step,
one more small step. Take it.
 I'll do the multiplication.

Moses Supposes

Moses supposes his toeses are roses,
but Moses supposes erroneously;
for nobody's toeses are posies of roses,
as Moses supposes his toeses to be.

That anonymous poem titled "Moses" appears in the delightful book, *A Family of Poems: My Favorite Poetry for Children* by Caroline Kennedy.

Supposing "Moses" is named after Moses of the Bible, I found myself looking for spiritual application.

"Moses supposes." Apparently, Moses is steeped in his imagination as he thinks his "toeses are roses." Yet the writer tells us, "Moses supposes erroneously." That is, Moses is not correct in his thinking. He has grasped something that is false. In fact, according to the voice of the poem, "nobody's toeses are posies of roses." It's not true for the toeses of Moses, and it's not true for anyone else's.

But I'll give the fellow this much credit: Moses could have thought his toeses were any number of things besides roses. Unhealthy images could have nestled in his head. So I compliment his imagination. In fact, I believe Moses holds onto a divine imagination. Roses are beautiful flowers in sight and scent. They are symbolic of love. They are symbolic of Mary, the mother of Jesus.

There are several references to divine "supposes" in the Bible. Followers of Christ are to think on things that are pure, lovely, admirable, noble, true, right, excellent, and praiseworthy (Phil. 4:8 NIV). I remember these attributes by an acronym. The first letters of the eight words (in the order I've noted) spell "Plant Rep" (as in Plant Representative). While different translations present different adjectives, they're similar in nature; and each one speaks of a divine imagination.

On a similar note, we are to cast down anything that "sets itself up against the [true] knowledge of God" (2 Cor. 10:5a AMP). We are to throw out the false, the half-truth, the deceptive thought, and the disturbing image. We are to say "Good riddance!" to "god-images" that are not of Almighty God (Isa. 30:22 MSG). We are to set our minds "on the things above, not on the things that are on earth" (Col. 3:2). We're to bring "into captivity every thought to the obedience of Christ" (2 Cor. 10:5b KJV). We're to focus on "the simplicity and purity of devotion to Christ" (2 Cor. 11:3).

For some of us, thought life revision is a lifelong challenge. Some hurtful images are so steeped in our psyche, so familiar to our way of thinking that vital steps are needed to replace unhealthy thoughts with healthy thoughts. Through consistent and persistent focus on God's Word, we keep ourselves on the "Plant Rep" path. We don't conform to the world; we become "transformed by the renewing" of our minds (Rom. 12:2). We ditch the distorted for the divine, as we hoist ourselves onto the highway of holiness (Isa. 35:8 KJV).

In *Light in My Darkest Night*, Catherine Marshall (1914-1983) linked clean thoughts with "a healing of the whole woman." It's as though she were writing my own words as she confessed a need for "a real cleansing of my subconscious. So much debris, so much negativism, so many fear thoughts, so many thoughts of non-acceptance by God have piled up." Later, she adds:

> Our thought and imaginative life provides the building blocks out of which our souls and spirits are built. They are either nourished and grown in the knowledge and love of God, or else they atrophy and die. God means for us to look at the good, the beautiful, the true, the pure.

Author, speaker, and life coach Lynda Elliott agrees. She writes in

An Invitation To Healing, "His Word shows us how to remove any blocks that may keep us from receiving from Him." Of equal importance "we must keep our hearts and minds ready to hear His word of correction or direction."

Thought-enriching promises of "correction or direction" saturate God's Word. Yet, one may ask, what promises? Here are a few:

> People with their minds set on you [God], you keep completely whole, steady on their feet, because they keep at it and don't quit (Isa. 26:3 MSG).

> Love . . . thinks no evil (1 Cor. 13:4, 5 NKJV).

> For God is at work within you, helping you want to obey him, and then helping you do what he wants (Phil. 2:13 TLB).

> Keep putting into practice all you learned from me [the Apostle Paul] and heard from me and saw me doing, and the God of peace will be with you (Phil. 4:9 NLT).

> [God] is a rewarder of them that diligently seek him (Heb. 11:6 KJV).

These are promises worthy of an attitude of gratitude.

Throughout the day, what are we supposing? Are we supposing speculations short on truth? Or statements full of truth? May I suggest: We remember that we are a product of God's imagination, not our own (Ps. 100:3). We are made "in the likeness of God" (Gen. 5:1). He's the producer, the builder, the manufacturer, the image-maker. And God's Son, Jesus, came on earth to model God's divine image for us. As Catherine Marshall wrote, "God is never finished with a man until he is conformed to the image of His Son."

It is no "supposing erroneously;" it is divine truth: Followers of Christ "have the mind of Christ" (1 Cor. 2:16), including His imagination. Yet, as God did not speak to Moses at the burning bush until Moses turned aside to look (Exod. 3:3-4), we must turn our thoughts toward the pure, lovely, admirable, noble, true, right, excellent, and praiseworthy in order to keep ourselves from supposing erroneously. Then we, the "fragrance of Christ" (2 Cor. 2:15)—changed into His image "from glory to glory" (2 Cor. 3:18) "by the manifestation of truth" (2 Cor. 4:2)—will know "the Mighty One has done great things" (Luke 1:49), as we hold onto a divine imagination, standing among "posies of roses" with Moses on holy ground (Exod. 3:5).

My Leather Chaps

Stand, therefore, having your loins
girded about with truth . . . (EPH. 6:14 KJV).

The scripture above reminds me of *having my legs girded about with chaps* for the hometown rodeo forty years ago. As a participant in the annual rodeo and parade in Crossett, Arkansas, my western ensemble included *chaps*: "leather leggings joined by a belt or lacing, often having flared outer flaps, and worn over the trousers" (*Merriam-Webster's Collegiate Dictionary*).

The rodeo parade was held on a Wednesday afternoon in the month of August. There were marching bands, floats, convertibles, and hundreds of riders on horses. The local police blocked off the traffic, and we covered a lot of territory. The highlight was Main Street, where most of the crowd gathered on the long sidewalks with their cameras, sunglasses, paper fans, and popsicles. For the out-of-town guests, brightly-colored welcome signs, along with tempera-painted caricatures of cowboys, clowns, Brahma bulls, and broncos appeared on the store-front windows, including my dad's jewelry store.

Wednesday through Saturday nights at 8 o'clock sharp, it was *standing room only* at Cap Gates Arena for the start of the Crossett Rodeo, produced by sixteen-time World Champion Cowboy, Jim Shoulders. As I rode my horse in the Grand Entry those four summer nights, I stood tall in the saddle in my leather chaps, with the Crossett Riding Club's logo sewn on the lower leggings: a red horseshoe arched over a green pine tree. As a teenage cowgirl—and, if I may add, the 1967 Rodeo Queen of Farmerville, Louisiana—I was *hot stuff* in high western fashion when the rodeo rolled into town.

Maybe it's because I wore my leather chaps for such a short season, but this cowgirl distinctly remembers—pre-parade and pre-Grand Entry—standing in front of a full-length mirror, buckling my chaps at the waist and around the back of my new Wrangler® blue jeans. If I did not fasten the buckles, the chaps would toss back and forth as I rode my quarter-horse, a light-colored buckskin named Scooter.

Similarly, when we don't have our "loins girded about with truth" (Eph. 6:14), we are like "infants, tossed back and forth . . . , blown here and there by every wind of teaching" and "deceitful scheming" that is not of God (Eph. 4:14 NIV). Clearly, there are dangers in *knowing* God's truth but not *applying* it to our home on the range lives (2 Tim. 3:5-7); like my putting on leather chaps but not securing them to my body. On the other hand, a sound body (individually or collectively) greatly profits from applying God's truth in our everyday lives.

While specific western wear, such as *chaparajos*, might not appear in the Bible, there is a story about a linen sash wrapped around a man's waist. In Jeremiah 13:1-11, God instructs the prophet Jeremiah to put a linen sash around his waist, go to a riverbank, and hide the sash in a hole in a rock. Many days later—upon Jeremiah's retrieving the sash as God tells him to do—the sash is ruined, "profitable for nothing" (Jer. 13:7 NKJV). The LORD compares this story to the consequences of disobedience:

> Thus says the LORD: "In this manner I will ruin the pride of Judah and the great pride of Jerusalem. This evil people, who refuse to hear My words, who follow the dictates of their hearts, and walk after other gods to serve them and worship them, shall be just like this sash which is profitable for nothing. For as the sash clings to the waist of a man, so I have caused the whole house of Israel and the whole house of Judah to cling to Me," says the LORD, "that they may become My people, for renown, for praise, and for glory; but they would not hear" (JER. 13:9-11 NKJV).

Another prophet, Isaiah, describes a belt, soon to be worn by a brilliant man named Jesus: "Righteousness shall be the belt of His loins, and faithfulness the belt of His waist" (Isa. 11:5 NKJV).

Buckaroos: Whether we ride that pony on the warning of Jeremiah or the foresight of Isaiah, I believe it is clear: God wants us to apply His Word in our daily lives; to be righteous and faithful to Him and Him alone. Not just hear the Word of God and toss it off (Matt. 13:4, 19), like a green ranch-hand fresh out of the chute, quick to be tossed off the back of a bucking Appaloosa. Rather, put the Word of God into practice (James 1:22), like a seasoned saint, in record-breaking time roping, tying, and throwing the devil to the dirt; and lifting holy hands to his Maker (1 Tim. 2:8).

We are to gird our loins with truth (Eph. 6:14). We are to wrap the Word of God around us. We are to stand (Eph. 6:11).

The cleaving of an article of clothing to one's body—be that a pair of leather chaps, a linen sash, or a belt—is a picture of how the LORD wants us to be: closely knit to the World-Champion Producer of Life; standing firm, holding fast, buckled down to the task at hand, reigning in His parade, wrapped in His arms of love: That we may become the LORD's people "for renown, for praise, and for glory" (Jer. 13:11 NKJV).

My New Word

Do you have a new word? One you have seen on the printed page or heard someone say, but you don't know the meaning of it? On more than one occasion, I remember Mother, Shirley Elliott Scisson, (1922-1998) telling me: "If you don't know the meaning of a word, look it up."

The occasion of my new word was an out-of-state wedding, which called for my getting directions to the various events, including the bridal luncheon held at an elegant country club secured by a gated entrance. The gatekeeper's directions were to drive through a tree-lined boulevard, pass a few buildings on the left and right, and go up to the . . . unfamiliar word. He said the word so fast that I did not catch it, and I was too embarrassed to ask a second time. The passengers in my car were equally stumped. Mercy prevailed. We reached our destination, thanks to recognizing and following the cars ahead of us.

But what had the gatekeeper said?

At table among a circle of relatives, I confessed my ignorance over the unfamiliar word. After all, we're family. I told them it was a long word; I thought the first syllable was "port," but I did not think it was "portico" because I heard more than three syllables. One relative, who likes to get a laugh, said the gatekeeper probably said to "drive up to the Porta Potties." While laughter is good medicine, I remained clueless over my new word. Another relative, who teaches history, comes to the rescue. Not only does she know the word, she pronounces and spells it correctly. How would I know? The minute I got home, I looked it up and confirmed her response.

My new word: *porte cochère* [pôrt kō'SHE(ə)r]. The *New Oxford American Dictionary* defines a *porte cochère* as "a covered entrance large enough for vehicles to pass through." It is "a porch where vehicles stop to discharge passengers." The word goes back to the late seventeenth century; it's French and literally means "coach gateway."

I have gone bonkers over my new word. If you find a more elegant word, please let me know, especially one with so many spiritual applications. Think about it: God longs for us to come under His *porte cochère* (Ps. 91:1-4). It is a safe place of refined grace.

I imagine some theologians would call God's *porte cochère*: the blood of Jesus, relying on scriptures, such as these:

God has given us eternal life, and this life is in His Son
(1 JOHN 5:11).

. . . and from Jesus Christ . . . To Him who loves us and
released us from our sins by His blood—and He has made us
to be a kingdom . . . (REV. 1:5-6).

Others might focus on the Holy Spirit (John 14:16), stating while Jesus lived on earth for thirty-three years, the Holy Spirit has been working on earth for over two thousand years. "I [Jesus Christ] will ask the Father, and He will give you another Helper [the Holy Spirit], that He may be with you forever" (John 14:16).

Have you come under the *porte cochère* of Almighty God, who desires all of us "to be saved and to come to the knowledge of the truth" (1 Tim. 2:4)? Have you considered the blood of Jesus that enables us to "come boldly unto the throne of grace" (Heb. 4:16 KJV)—to move from the porch to the main building, if you will; from the outer tabernacle to the inner (Heb. 9:6-7; 6:19-20)? Or has someone or some thing tripped you up, and you're stuck . . . like in a closed, dimly lit garage with no exit in sight? *Porte cochère* could become your new word and open up your new world: the Kingdom of God with Jesus as your Savior and Champion (Isa. 19:20).

For others, elsewhere on their spiritual journey, questions like these might surface:

Among the gatekeepers of our souls (pastor, counselor, mentor, or sponsor), have we been too embarrassed to confess we are directionally impaired (Matt. 23:37b; Gal. 1:6-7)?

Have we fallen into idolatry, legalism, prayerlessness, pride, or unbelief?

Have we grieved or quenched the Holy Spirit
(Eph. 4:30; 1 Thess. 5:19)?

Have we settled for the good life and failed to pursue the great life?

Whether we're in a season of goodness or greatness, discovery or recovery, kingdom birth or kingdom building, do we hear the Spirit call? Calling us to partake of blessings far wider in scope than valet-parking under a *porte cochère*. Calling us to know the fullness of God as Father, Son, and Holy Spirit. Calling us to live in the "precious and magnificent promises" (2 Pet. 1:4) of our gracious Lord. Calling us to be the Bride of Christ (2 Cor. 11:2-3; Rev. 19:7, 22:17).

27

Near The Firelight

In the middle of the courtyard
near the firelight, I see a face familiar.
I take a closer look.
I say to my pals, "This man was with him."
Quickly he smarts off, "Woman, I don't know him!"
Well, I might be just a servant girl
but he's lying through his teeth.
I tell him off: "Yeah, yeah,
you followed that Jesus man
while things were going well,
but now that he's arrested
all the likes of you
will fade like withered grass."

Mid-afternoon, a month later,
I see this same smarty pants
standing in the spotlight.
They say his name is Peter.
He heals the old crippled beggar,
one of the likes of me.
Peter talks a different talk:
"By faith in the name of Jesus,
this man who you see and know
was made strong. It is Jesus' name

and the faith that comes through him
that has given this complete healing to him."

Not a bit in front of my friends
do I show my emotions,
but deep inside I can't deny
I'm taken back. Is this
the same man who denied his Jesus?
This, I've got to think about:
Don't tell my friends
but if Peter healed the crippled beggar,
maybe he will heal
a crippled girl like me
and I'll be a servant to his Jesus, a sister
to the man I mocked a month ago
seated there near the firelight.

[Based on Luke 22:55-57; Acts 3:1-16]

Our Founding Father

God is our Founding Father in the spiritual realm, like George Washington is our nation's Founding Father in the political realm. Among other names, our God is known as "The Alpha" (the beginning or first in Rev.1:8, 11; 21:6; 22:13), "The Ancient of Days" (Dan. 7:9, 13, 22), and our "Father" (Luke 11:2, among others). So, we could easily say God is our Founding Father.

At the Arkansas Arts Center in Little Rock in May 2004, I saw the original "Lansdowne" portrait of George Washington by Gilbert Stuart. As I viewed the magnificent work, painted over 200 years ago, I drew spiritual comparisons by the handfuls. Here's a thimble-full:

From information provided by the National Portrait Gallery's Exhibition Tour on "George Washington: A National Treasure," I learned that, in 1796, Washington sat for the portrait only long enough for the artist to paint his face. Then, Gilbert Stuart was left to his imagination to depict Washington's pose. The artist chose to clothe Washington in a suit of black velvet, to quote the exhibition, "dignified and solemn . . . elegant but simple."

In contrast, our Savior and Lord Jesus, while living on earth, had "no stately form or majesty that we should look upon Him, nor appearance that we should be attracted to Him" (Isa. 53:2). Furthermore, during His earthly life, Jesus "was despised and forsaken of men, a man of sorrows, and acquainted with grief" (Isa. 53:3).

Yet, several chapters earlier, this same prophet, Isaiah, portrays Jesus in a *different* setting—where Jesus is in heaven with Father God.

In fact, Isaiah has a visual experience of incredible majesty. Isaiah "saw the Lord seated on a throne, high and exalted, and the train of His robe filled the temple" (Isa. 6:1 NIV). And the New Testament enhances the picture with this stroke of the brush: Jesus Christ "has sat down at the right hand of the throne of God" (Heb. 12:2).

Like Stuart's full-length portrait of Washington, the inspired writers of the Bible portray what Father God and Jesus look like. In Revelation 1:13, the disciple John's vision depicts Jesus, in heaven, as being:

> Dressed in a robe reaching down to his feet and with a golden sash around his chest. His head and hair were white like wool, as white as snow, and his eyes were like blazing fire. His feet were like bronze glowing in a furnace, and his voice was like the sound of rushing waters. In his right hand he held seven stars, and out of his mouth came a sharp double-edged sword. His face was like the sun shining in all its brilliance
> (REV. 1:13-16 NIV).

A similar vision of God appears in the Book of Daniel:

> The Ancient of Days took his seat. His clothing was as white as snow; the hair of his head was white like wool. His throne was flaming with fire, and its wheels were all ablaze. A river of fire was flowing, coming out from before him. Thousands upon thousands attended him; ten thousand times ten thousand stood before him. . . . (DAN. 7:9-10 NIV).

A few verses later, Daniel shows us *another* figure in the picture with our "Ancient of Days" God:

> In my vision at night I looked, and there before me was one like a son of man [Jesus], coming with the clouds of heaven. He approached the Ancient of Days [God, the Father] and was led into his presence (DAN. 7:13 NIV).

And there are more awe-inspiring visions to read about at Daniel 10:5-6 and Ezekiel 1:1, 26-28.

The "Lansdowne" portrait of Washington—unlike Stuart's "Athenaeum" portrait that appears on the American $1 bill—is head to toe, full-length on a canvas that is 95 by 60 inches, emphasizing Washington's importance as a statesman. Did you realize *all* eyes will see Jesus when He returns full-length? "All the nations of the earth" will "see the Son of Man coming on the clouds of the sky, with power and great glory" (Matt. 24:30 NIV). And Revelation 1:7 paints the same extraordinary masterpiece: "Look, He [Jesus] is coming with the clouds, and every eye will see him . . ." (Rev. 1:7 NIV).

In the "Lansdowne" oil on canvas portrait of Washington, other than Washington's face, the rest of his body is based on that of a stand-in employed by the artist. Aren't we, as believers, called to "stand-in" for Jesus as His "ambassadors" (2 Cor. 5:20)? Or, as Paul compliments believers in Thessalonica, "You became imitators of us and of the Lord . . ." (1 Thess. 1:6 NIV). And Paul carries the same message to the Corinthians: "Be imitators of me, just as I also am of Christ" (1 Cor. 11:1).

Like George Washington's remarkable deeds over two hundred years ago, as well as those of "so great a cloud of witnesses surrounding us" (Heb.12:1), may we let our "good deeds shine out for all to see, so that everyone will praise [our] heavenly Father" (Matt. 5:15-16 NLT). After all, our Founding Father, better known as "The Alpha," "The Ancient of Days," and simply "Father," stands for everything that is good. In fact, "every good and perfect gift is from above, coming down from the Father of the heavenly lights" (James 1:17 NIV).

[See "Lansdowne" portrait of George Washington by Gilbert Stuart online at *http://georgewashington.si.edu/portrait/index.html*.]

Pleasant Words

God prefers pleasant words over painful words (Prov. 16:24). Words that heal, not wound; words that build up, not tear down. "Let your speech always be with grace, seasoned with salt, that you may know how you ought to answer each one" (Col. 4:6 NKJV). In other words, I'm not to pepper the atmosphere with "unwholesome words" (Eph. 4:29) or what is generally considered offensive language.

God emphasizes His point: He connects pleasant words with life itself. "Death and life are in the power of the tongue, and those who live it will eat its fruit" (Prov. 18:21).

It's not so much a matter of allowing God to control my tongue. It's a matter of allowing Him to change my heart: "For out of the abundance of the heart" my "mouth speaks" (Luke 6:45 NKJV). If good is in my heart, good will come out of my mouth. If not-so-good, I need spiritual heart surgery that the LORD is willing to perform:

> "I [the LORD] will give them an undivided heart and put a new
> spirit in them; I will remove from them their heart of stone and
> give them a heart of flesh" (EZEK. 11:19 NIV).

Let's face it: Life is hard. The daily grind does indeed grind. We are going to get frustrated, annoyed, and disappointed. It's not a matter of exercising self-control over my tongue *if* I get upset. It's a matter of exercising self-control *when* I get upset. In these instances, it's far easier to say something sharp or swift that is offensive to God—and supposedly stress-reducing—rather than find an appropriate verbal volley, such as: "by gum," "dog gone it," "for crying out loud," "good grief," or "great day in the morning."

Beth Moore tells us, "The Holy Spirit can use our tongues as instruments or vessels of supernatural power and can bring about stunning results, whether immediately or over time." I had never thought of my tongue as an instrument. One instrument I'm fond of is the piano. So, I ask myself—figuratively speaking—how will I play "my piano" today? Best I pray:

> Lord, help me to play my piano in a way that honors You. Help me to soft-pedal my remarks when I am frustrated, annoyed, or disappointed. Convict me, Lord, when I speak "worldly and empty chatter" for Your Word tells me that it only leads to more ungodliness and spreads "like gangrene" (2 TIM. 2:16-17). Help me to guard my tongue (PS. 39:1). May I not misuse Your Holy Name (EXOD. 20:7). I ask for an "undivided heart" (EZEK. 11:19), a "clean heart" (PS. 51:10) that enables me to make a sweet melody unto You (EPH. 5:19). May I glorify You, Father God, with the words that I speak. And thank You, Lord, for Your loving-kindnesses and compassions that "are new every morning" (LAM. 3:22-23). In the name of Jesus. Amen.

Truly, this instrument can be in tune with God's desires or out of tune.

God's Word says, "Like apples of gold in settings of silver is a word spoken in right circumstances" (Prov. 25:11). That takes me back to several years ago after learning of the death of a mentor. In the midst of my grieving, I shared memories of this saint with a friend over lunch about how I had been encouraged and exhorted on numerous occasions through the last decade and a half. As we got up from the table, I posed my final remark in the form of a question. "How can I best honor the memory of one now walking on 'a street of pure gold'?" (Rev. 21:21).

Her grace-filled, "apples of gold in settings of silver" response? "Live well."

What do you say? No matter what life rolls our way, let's have a great day in the morning. Let's speak the best words we can with a finely-tuned instrument: wholesome words that bless and build up; pleasant words that heal and nurture; words "sweet to the soul and healing to the bones" (Prov. 16:24); words that speak LIFE—through the power of the resurrection of Jesus Christ (John 11:25-26)!

Prayer for Pastors
and the Priesthood of Believers

Father God, in the name of Jesus and by the power of the Holy Spirit, I pray for Your pastors: those You have called to watch over our souls (Heb. 13:17). Thank You, Father, for pastors and all those who have spoken the Word of God to my family, my friends, my city, and to me (Heb. 13:7).

Father, I ask that you forgive me: for my sin of omission in not praying more often for pastors (Eph. 6:19; Col. 4:3). Forgive me, Lord, for taking them for granted. Forgive me for my lack of fervency in praying for those in authority over me (1 Tim. 2:1-5; Heb. 13:18-19). I confess, Father, that my sin of omission is something that I am to correct, as Your Word commands (2 Chron. 7:14; Ps. 139:23-24).

Father God, now, with the assurance that my sin is forgiven—and thank You that it is—I lift up the pastors of my city and my state. I ask that You minister to them: the beauty of holiness (Ps. 29:2 NKJV). Restore unto them the joy of Your salvation and sustain them with a willing spirit (Ps. 51:12); as it's Your joy that helps them to lead others to salvation (Ps. 51:13). May Your pastors *not* be grieved, but may they experience the joy of the LORD as their strength (Neh. 8:10; Eph. 6:10). And Father, if their hope has turned to disappointment, may they know that their hope is being purified (James 1:4; 1 John 3:3; Phil. 3:10). Help them in times of pain and uncertainty to call upon You (Ps. 50:15).

Lord, help Your pastors to keep the faith (Heb. 11:6)—to walk in the faith that they profess (Heb. 4:14, 10:26 KJV; John 5:14 GNT). Help them to practice righteousness (1 John 2:29, 3:10). Remind them that obedience is better than sacrifice (1 Sam. 15:22-23). Help them to handle the Word of God with honor (2 Cor. 4:2; Neh. 8:5). Remind them and their congregations that God's judgment begins with the household of God (1 Pet. 4:17); and teachers "will incur a stricter judgment" (James 3:1). May Your pastors keep in mind the necessity to proclaim the whole counsel and purpose of God (Acts 20:26-27; Ezek. 33:6). May Your pastors—as well as all in the "priesthood of believers" (1 Pet. 2:9; Gal. 3:28)—write God's commandments on the tablet of our hearts (Prov. 7:2-3).

Father, as Jesus increased in wisdom (Luke 2:52), may Your pastors learn more of You (2 Tim. 3:7; 2 Pet. 1:8; Hosea 4:6; Col. 1:9-10); and exercise Your power (1 Thess. 1:5; 2 Pet. 1:3). May they hold onto *all* of Your promises, rather than a portion or a mere form of godliness (2 Tim. 3:5). May the truth be affirmed and the false discerned (2 Tim. 3:15).

Lord, I ask that Your pastors persevere (Gal. 5:1). Help them to keep Your commandments: so they will abide in Your love *and* have supernatural joy that is full, complete, and overflowing (John 15:10-11 NKJV). Remind Your pastors of their holy calling (Rom. 8:28; 1 Cor. 12:28 AMP); remind them of the eternal rewards that wait for them (see Rev. 1, 2, 3). Help them to be above reproach (1 Tim. 3:1-7). May they love what is good, sensible, just, and devout. May they exhort in sound doctrine, not false doctrine (1 Thess. 2:3; 1 Tim. 1:3; 2 Tim. 4:3-4). May they refute those who contradict sound doctrine (Titus 1:7-9). May they bear much fruit (John 15:8, 16; Gal. 5:22-23), as Your pastors are "more than conquerors" through Christ Jesus who loves them (Rom. 8:37 NKJV).

Help Your pastors to be humble and pray, rather than proud and self-sufficient (2 Chron. 7:13-14). Remind them of Your promise: that if they ask for things in the Name of Jesus, they will receive, so that their joy may be made full (John 16:24). Lord, I ask that no root of bitterness spring up that causes trouble (Heb. 12:15-16; Ps. 46:10). Help Your pastors to deny themselves, take up the cross, and follow Jesus Christ (Matt. 16:24). Help them to escape the corruption that is in the world by lust (2 Pet. 1:4; 1 Pet. 1:14-16, 2:11; Jude 18). May they be partakers of the divine nature (2 Pet. 1:4). Encourage Your pastors, Father, with this promise: that Christ lives in them (Gal. 2:20; Col. 1:27). And they live and move and have their being in Christ (Acts 17:28 KJV; Phil. 3:9). And thank you, Father God, for Your promise: to provide a way of escape from temptation (1 Cor. 10:13; Heb. 4:15). Thank You, God, that You are faithful (1 Cor. 10:13; Jude 24; 1 Thess. 5:24; 2 Tim. 2:13).

Heavenly Father, protect Your pastors from embracing "a different gospel" (Gal. 1:6, Col. 2:18). Deliver Your pastors from "enemies of the cross of Christ . . . who set their minds on earthly things" (Phil. 3:19; Col. 3:2). Deliver Your pastors and their congregations from any worship of idols (Col. 3:5; 1 Thess. 1:9). Father, discipline with Your righteousness anyone in Your church who tries to persuade others to believe or act on things that are unbiblical (Jude 4; 2 Cor. 10:5, 11:3). As Your Word says it would be better for a millstone to be hung around one's neck and they drown in the sea, than to cause one of Your little ones to stumble (Matt. 18:6-7).

Protect Your pastors from troublemakers: those who oppose the teaching of sound doctrine (2 Tim. 4:15; Heb. 13:9). Protect them from boastful and rebellious men and women; from empty talkers, deceitful workers, imposters, and those who, by smooth words, turn to godlessness (1 Titus 1:10-11; Dan. 11:32). Rescue Your pastors from perverse and evil men and women (2 Tim. 3:1-8). Almighty God, protect them from all evil.

Father, may Your pastors live such good lives that when others accuse them of doing wrong, their good deeds are clearly evident (1 Pet. 2:12). Father, I speak peace to their hearts in times of persecution. Cover them with the blood of Jesus. And in the name of Jesus, I speak angelic safety to pastors and churches (Ps. 34:7). No weapon formed against them shall prosper (Is. 54:17). And the gates of hell shall not prevail against Your Church (Matt. 16:18 NKJV).

Help Your pastors in the preparation and delivery of Your messages, for Your Word says "the people who know their God will display strength and take action" (Dan. 11:32). Encourage them, Father, to lift up the name of Jesus (John 12:33). Help them to make known with boldness the mystery of the gospel (Eph. 6:19). Give them an extra measure of energy. Give them a strong support team (Exod. 17:11-12;

Acts 6:2-4). Help them to be salt and light (Matt. 5:13-14).

Give Your pastors favor with their flock (Luke 2:52). I bind a spirit of lethargy, complacency, and apathy off the pastors and off the members of their congregations, in the name of Jesus (Matt. 16:19, 18:18; Phil. 2:9-11). By Your Holy Spirit, help them to guard the treasure which has been entrusted to them (2 Tim. 1:14). May their churches be houses of prayer (Luke 19:46) and "the pillar and support of the Truth" (1 Tim. 3:15).

Lord, I ask that You give abundantly to Your pastors the gifts of Your Holy Spirit: the Spirit of wisdom, understanding, knowledge, and any other gift as You see fit (1 Cor. 12, 14). Like the sons of Issachar, may they understand the times with knowledge of what they should do (1 Chron. 12:32). Give them wisdom in matters of church discipline (Matt. 18:15-17; Titus 1:13, 3:10; Jude 22-23). Help Your pastors to minister as true servants of Jesus Christ and stewards of Your divine mysteries (Col. 1:26, 4:3; 1 Tim. 3:16). Remind them that they are on the winning side with Jesus Christ, the "Lord of lords and King of kings," and those who are with Him "are the called and chosen and faithful" (Rev. 17:14).

Father, provide for the needs of Your pastors: emotional, financial, mental, physical, and spiritual. Help them to cast all their anxiety on You, Father, because You care for them (1 Pet. 5:7). Help them to balance their lives. Guard their hearts. Guard their conduct (Heb. 13:18). Guard their thoughts (Phil. 4:8). Guard their marriages, their families, their homes, and all they hold dear. Father God, in the name of Jesus, heal Your pastors. Love Your pastors; because You, God, are love (1 John 4:8).

May they grow in grace, grow in good works, and grow in holiness (Heb. 13:21; Jude 20; 2 Pet. 1:5-11; Col. 2:19; Isa. 54:2; 1 Chron. 4:10). Guide them, Father, into Your peace and Your rest (Eph. 2:14; Col. 3:15; 2 Thess. 3:16; Heb. 4:9). Give Your pastors a supernatural manifestation that You are Lord. You are their Shepherd; and goodness and kindness shall follow them all the days of their lives, and they will dwell in the house of the LORD forever (Psalm 23:6).

In the name of Jesus, amen.

Question on Second Chronicles 7:14

"If my people, who are called by my name,
shall humble themselves, and pray,
and seek my face, and turn from their wicked ways,
then will I hear from heaven, and will forgive their sin,
and will heal their land" (2 CHRON. 7:14 KJV).

When God says to turn from our wicked ways (2 Chron. 7:14), what does He mean by "wicked"? I think I'm feeling condemned.

In this verse, "wicked" is used as an adjective, not a noun. Yet, it is a *strong* adjective, and I can't mince words: Wicked means "bad" or "evil." And this is what I am to turn from: anything that is bad or evil.

I also see in Baker and Carpenter's *The Complete Word Study Dictionary, Old Testament* that there are "various shades" of meaning "according to its contextual usage." The word "can be used to attribute a negative aspect to nearly anything" . . . that is "displeasing," "disagreeable, unwholesome, or harmful." I'm to stop making *displeasing* remarks. I'm to change my *disagreeable* attitude. I'm to part from an *unwholesome* activity. I'm to avoid a *harmful* substance. These various shades of wicked ways: God commands I turn from.

Why?

Because rays of righteousness—things that are pleasing, agreeable, wholesome, and helpful—attract God's presence. Shades of sin do not. That is, wicked ways are not in my best interest. My sense of peace is diminished when I participate, whole-heartedly or half-heartedly, in anything that God says is bad or evil. Secondly, my relationships are affected. Third, Romans 8:22 says "all of creation groans over the weight [impact or consequences] of sin." If I don't identify, confess, and turn from wicked ways, the land is negatively affected: the air I breathe, the water I drink, the birds, the trees, the fish in the sea, the stars in the sky, the people on earth. As I have looked at 2 Chronicles 7:13-14 repeatedly these past few days, I don't believe that's a grandiose statement. I think I'm connecting the right dots. I am part of the cosmos. I am part of God's creation. I am part of Christ's body. My sins, individually and corporately, have a negative impact on *all* of creation, and my righteousness through Jesus Christ has a positive impact. "So it shall be . . . the blessing and the curse which I [the LORD] have set before you . . ." (Deut. 30:1).

Finally, consider the source of my feelings. Condemnation is from the devil (John 10:10; Rev. 12:10). Conviction is from God. While God disciplines those He loves (Heb. 12:6), God is not suggesting in this verse, nor any other, that I am wicked [as a noun]. God forbid. My essence, my identity, my make-up as a child of God—"a new creation" (2 Cor. 5:17 NIV), a daughter of the "Lord of lords and King of kings" (Rev. 17:14), a follower of Jesus Christ—is closely linked to the Light of the World. I am part of a "royal priesthood" (1 Pet. 2:9) and "the hope of glory" (Col. 1:27). My citizenship is in heaven (Phil. 3:20). And "His banner over me is love" (Song of Sol. 2:4).

Raindrops

haiku: "an unrhymed verse form of Japanese origin
having three lines containing usually five, seven and
five syllables, respectively."
(*Merriam-Webster's*)

Raindrops on my roof
remind me of God's sweet peace
and takes me to sleep.

Saul's Conversion

Before his conversion, a picture of Saul, later known as Paul (Acts 13:9), shows him watching, with consent, the stoning of Stephen, the first Christian martyr (Acts 7:58). A second picture reveals Saul's plan to find and imprison Christians, as he and his entourage jaunt to Damascus with that sole purpose in mind (Acts 8:3, 9:1-3, 22:4-6, 26:10-13).

But God the Father, Son, and Holy Spirit had other things in mind, which is an understatement when we consider a vast portion of the New Testament was later written by this same individual. In fact, Saul's transformation is so profound that after conversion, he greatly encourages Christ followers (Acts 22:14-15), addressing them with terms of endearment, such as "my beloved brethren . . . my joy and crown" (Phil. 4:1).

Let's enter the divine drama.

"As Saul was coming near the city of Damascus, suddenly a light from the sky flashed around him" (Acts 9:3 GNT).

Notice that Saul was not far from Damascus. He was nearly there; he was close to his goal. Don't you imagine Christians in Damascus were praying that God protect them from persecutors like Saul (Acts 9:13)? God answers their prayers, but He waits until Saul is close at hand. I'm reminded of the saying, "God is never on time, but He's never late."

Quite unexpectedly, Jesus enters the scene as a light from heaven flashes all around. This is Saul's moment: his change point, his high point, his encounter with the Light of the World (John 8:12), also known as the Bright Morning Star (Revelation 22:16). Saul falls to the ground and hears "a voice saying to him: 'Saul, Saul! Why do you per-secute Me?'" (Acts 9:4 GNT).

Notice that angels do not transport Saul to the nearest mountain top, where Jesus transfigures him in the midst of thunder rolls and lightning bolts. No, not at all. We see Saul down in the dust, ground-ed by the Almighty, in on the ground floor of Christianity 101.

The first words that Jesus says to Saul demonstrate mercy to the dig-nity of the man, who was created in God's image (Gen. 1:26-27, 2:7). The Lord addresses Saul by his name, not once but twice: "Saul, Saul!"

Then the Prince of Peace drops a most important question: "Why do you persecute Me?" Jesus did not ask, "Why do you persecute My followers?" He asks, "Why do you persecute *Me*?" (Acts 9:4 GNT, emphasis added; see also Matt. 10:40). Jesus knows Saul better than Saul knows himself. Our "Wonderful Counselor" (Isa. 9:6) knows why Saul persecutes, but Jesus wants Saul to see that for himself.

Like a wrinkle in time, instantly God has touched the core of this man's heart. No way around it: it was high impact at high noon (Acts 22:6, 26:13). Yet, Saul was not converted into a god or a centaur-like crea-ture out of *The Chronicles of Narnia: The Lion, The Witch and The Wardrobe*. Saul keeps his humanity and his personality. In a state of total bewilderment, the grounded and blinded man answers the Lord's question, "Why do you persecute Me?" with a question: "Who are you, Lord?" (Acts 9:5).

How does Saul know that he is talking to the Lord Jehovah, rather than a counterfeit spirit, an "angel of light" in disguise? (2 Cor. 11:13-14). The fact that Saul calls Him "Lord" confirms that Jesus has instant-ly revealed two key elements of His character: (1) supernatural truth: Saul suddenly knows who is in his midst: none other than the "Lord of lords and King of kings" (Rev. 17:14); and (2) supernatural power: Saul was literally thrown to the ground, blinded by a bright light as way of introduction to the Almighty (Acts 22:6-11).

Furthermore, Saul asks, "Who are you, Lord?" because if Saul truly knew the Lord, he would not persecute the Lord, nor His disci-ples (Acts 26:6-9). Is that why the Old Testament tells us, "My people are destroyed for lack of knowledge" (Hosea 4:6)? Is that why the New Testament tells us, "When anyone hears the word of the kingdom and does not understand it, the evil one comes and snatches away what has been sown in his heart" (Matt. 13:19)? No wonder Solomon prayed for "an understanding heart" over everything else (1 Kings 3:5-10).

Jesus answers Saul's question, "Who are you, Lord?" by identifying His name: "I am Jesus . . ." (Acts 9:5). But Jesus loves Saul too much to leave it at that. Jesus reveals the immediate source of holy contention, guiding the man out of denial: ". . . whom you persecute" (Acts 9:5). After all, "faithful are the wounds of a friend" (Prov. 27:6).

The Lord's first instruction to Saul is "Get up and go into the city . . ." (Acts 9:6 GNT). Or, as they say in a recovery program: "Suit up and show up." Jesus offers more information: ". . . where you will be told what you must do" (Acts 9:6 GNT). God asks Saul to take his first step in faith with the promise that Saul will receive more instructions later.

Perhaps to Saul's regret and to ours, God does not reveal the entire game plan of Saul's future. Throughout scriptures, that is not God's mode of operation. "Give us *this day* our *daily* bread," we pray (Matt. 6:11, emphasis added). All that is told to Saul is to go into the city, and there he will be told vital information (Acts 9:6, 22:10). Nothing complicated; nothing beyond his ability; and Saul chooses to obey. Aren't we thankful that he obeyed?

Seeing Ourselves in Seabiscuit

"Do you [Job] give the horse his strength or clothe his neck with a flowing mane?

Do you make him leap like a locust, striking terror with his proud snorting?

He paws fiercely, rejoicing in his strength, and charges into the fray.

He laughs at fear, afraid of nothing; he does not shy away from the sword. . . .

In frenzied excitement he eats up the ground; he cannot stand still when the trumpet sounds" (JOB 39:19-24 NIV).

In Laura Hillenbrand's best-selling book, *Seabiscuit: An American Legend*—also a movie by the same title—I read that Seabiscuit "didn't run, he rampaged." And when any new rider "tried to rein him in, the horse bolted, thrashing around like a hooked marlin," habitually meeting every command with resistance—even "feeding off the fight and gaining satisfaction from the distress and rage of the man on his back."

Who hasn't occasionally been resistant, or at least complacent, to the Lord's desires and direction for our lives? Who hasn't, at one time or another, met the Lord's commands to obey Him with resistance, thrashing around in our selfish and misguided ways like a stubborn horse? And yet, our Sovereign Lord knows how to "get to us," just like Tom Smith, Seabiscuit's new trainer, knew how to handle this "train wreck" of a horse.

One method Smith used was he took "coercion out of the equation and let the horse discover the pleasure of speed." Seabiscuit had thoroughbred in his blood. The love of running, the pleasure of speed was in the horse's soul, and Smith let the horse discover that.

One way Smith let Seabiscuit "discover the pleasure of speed" was by calling out to the rider: "Let him go!" What probably seemed like a frustrating season for the horse's trainer, jockey, and owner, Seabiscuit would take off in the wrong direction, dipping and swerving all around the track, sometimes even hurdling the infield fence.

Yet, with Smith's specific instructions, the rider let Seabiscuit do just as he pleased, which reminds me of the prodigal son's "rampage" in a distant country far from home (Luke 15:12). Sometimes the Lord lets us—as prodigal sons and daughters—do our own thing, knowing with mere time and experience we will finally choose His Will for our lives. Smith let Seabiscuit choose what to do, just as God lets us have free will in our choices.

Did you discover that operative word, "let," which appears nine hundred times in the Bible, including two hundred times in the New Testament? A man *let* a horse discover the pleasure of speed. A man *let* a horse choose what to do, just like God *lets* us discover the pleasure of His promises.

Run these promises from the King James Version around the race track of your soul:

"Let not your heart be troubled, neither let it be afraid" (JOHN 14:27B).

Let this mind be in you, which was also in Christ Jesus (PHIL. 2:5).

Let the peace of God rule in your hearts . . . (COL. 3:15).

Let the Word of Christ dwell in you richly . . . (COL. 3:16).

Let us run with patience the race that is set before us (HEB. 12:1).

After weaving all over the track, the exhausted horse finally realized there "was nowhere to go but home," which reminds me of the prodigal child finally coming to his senses (Luke 15:18). Or the passage in John 6:66-68 where Jesus asks Peter where he will go now that the other disciples had left Jesus, and Peter replies: "Lord, to whom shall we go? You have words of eternal life."

Eventually, Seabiscuit was transformed "from a rogue to a pliant, happy horse." And "he would never again be forced to do what he didn't want to do." And what was the end result? Seabiscuit never again fought a rider and, in 1938, this undersized, crooked-legged racehorse became a champion, even to the point of surpassing the President of the United States, Franklin Delano Roosevelt, as the year's number-one newsmaker. From spending "nearly two seasons floundering in the lowest ranks of racing, misunderstood and mishandled," Seabiscuit became an American legend—thanks to an unlikely, but patient and persistent alliance: owner Charles Howard, trainer Tom Smith, and jockey Red Pollard.

Could revival within my soul and the souls of others happen with the right combination? What would that alliance look like? What trio would be called forth? Prayer, patience, and persistence? Or humility, hope, and help—reaching out for divine help and godly counsel—to tip the scales in God's favor?

Could our churches become packed with new faces because we choose to humble ourselves and cheer them on—in intercessory prayer and through practical measures—like the crowd at the race tracks in the 1930s cheered Seabiscuit on to victory?

A horse discovering the pleasure of speed and running like a champion. Men and women of faith discovering the pleasure of God's multiple promises and noting, among others, that His joy is our strength (Neh. 8:10).

Reference:
Hillenbrand, Laura. *Seabiscuit: An American Legend*. New York: Ballantine Publishing Group, a div. of Random House, 2001.

Table Manners

I have been known to resort to poor table manners if I don't know whether salt will come out of a shaker. I will cup my other hand, tilt the shaker over that empty hand, shake it, and see if any salt lands in the palm of my hand. If it does, I'll twist my wrist above my plate, knowing the law of gravity will cause the salt to fall. Then, I'll start shaking salt onto my food with—what I now know—is a functional utensil.

In Matthew 5:13, Jesus says that His followers are "the salt of the earth." Back in biblical times, salt was a scarce and sought-after product. "Salt money," or "salarium" in Latin, was the allowance of salt paid to soldiers in Rome. Our word "salary" is derived from the word salt. It is also a healing agent (2 Kings 2:21). The human body requires salt for regulation of fluid balance. Before refrigeration, salt was in high demand as a preservative. And its use today extends beyond the grocery store. Salt is used in ice control, in water softening, and in agricultural and industrial settings. Salt remains a valuable commodity.

There are over thirty references to salt in the Bible. In the Old Testament, salt was included in the meat offering sacrifice, because salt *made* the sacrifice good. That is, salt had a strong connection with the idea of a covenant relationship. Think of recipes. Just like salt literally makes a dish good and tasty, in the New Testament salt symbolically stands for the virtue or righteousness of Jesus Christ. God's covenant promise to us—the rich "seasoning" or "savor" of Christ's sacrifice on the cross to save us from our sins—is symbolically represented by salt.

"O taste and see that the LORD is good" (Ps. 34:8).

During His Sermon on the Mount, Jesus did not end His remarks on salt with: "You are the salt of the earth." He added a warning. "But if the salt has become tasteless, how can it be made salty again? It is no longer good for anything, except to be thrown out and trampled under foot by men" (Matt. 5:13). That's a trip from the grocery to the garbage.

The way I see this passage, I am to be salt without question. Regardless of what trial or temptation I'm going through. Regardless of my lame-blame excuses. Regardless of my attempts to rationalize why I think I should *give up* or *give in*. Such negative and faithless thoughts aren't worth a grain of salt in the eyes of my Lord, whose name is called "Wonderful Counselor, Mighty God, Eternal Father, Prince of Peace" (Isa. 9:6).

When I'm sprinkling the slightest of Christ-like salt to "one of the least of these" (Matt. 25:40), or I'm being faithful in a tiny window of opportunity (Luke 16:10), God is honored. God calls me not to *give up* and *give in* because I'm *give out*, but to keep on keeping on. I am to be salt. I am to add some measure of seasoning to the world that reflects the character of Jesus Christ. Not self-serving salt. Not compare-myself-to-Morton salt. Not toss-a-pinch-over-my-left-shoulder salt. Not sugar-in-the-salt shaker. I am to be *like* Jesus Christ. I am to conform to the standards that Jesus set during His tenure on earth. It's by learning who He is, cooperating with His commands, and obeying His teachings—through the power of the Holy Spirit—that enable me to be "the salt of the earth" (Matt. 5:13).

Jesus' *répondez s'il vous plaît* to be "the salt of the earth" invites us to walk in faith, even when the going gets tough. That reminds me of a spring day twenty-four years ago when I told a Christian woman—serving as a Titus 2:3 mentor—that if God did not answer my prayer request "by August 1, then I'm out of here; I'm chalking all this Christianity up to experience, and I'm leaving God."

Without hesitation, in a calm, non-threatening voice, this wise woman replied, "Linda, you might be through with God on August 1, but He won't be through with you."

Through an amazing attribute called the grace of God, at that unstable season in my life, I chose to "give ear," "take heed," and "hold fast" to what one with well-seasoned salt was telling me. In essence, the

Creator and sustainer of life is not going to let His daughter roam off His radar screen just because *her* expectations aren't being met in *her* timetable. Even when I'm not too pleased with how things are going, God is faithful (1 Cor. 10:13).

Besides salt being tied in with God's blessings, it is tied in with God's judgment. If my salt loses its savor through disobedience, the result is pitiful: I become a pillar of salt (Gen. 19:26). I am in danger of God's blessings being thrown out, and God's judgment coming up to the plate. The same salt that flavors and savors and even brings healing (ever gargle with salt water when you have a sore throat?) becomes something that is good for nothing, worthless, and barren.

Like rubbing salt in an open wound, my sacred text admittedly "stings" me here: "If salt has lost its taste—its strength, its quality—how can its saltiness be restored? It is not good for anything any longer but to be thrown out and trodden under foot by men" (Matt. 5:13 AMP).

Salt can be useful; salt can be useless. And so can I.

As a sprinkle of salt spreads its taste and flavor throughout a plate of food, may the teachings of Jesus Christ spread far and wide. After all, salt *of the earth* covers a lot more territory than salt *on a plate*. As we ask God to sprinkle our hearts clean from unrighteousness and help us to be the strong-quality salt that He desires, may we be encouraged that one day beyond this earthly life, we will join Him at a romantic "restaurant"—"candle-lit" by the glory of God (Rev. 21:23). Dining with the Divine in our best-of-best table manners, as this will be the Lord's table: "the marriage supper of the Lamb" (Rev. 19:9)—where His manner, His beauty, His grace go far beyond what eye has ever seen, what ear has ever heard (Isa. 64:4 KJV).

Take Away the Stone

Have you ever fretted over a prayer request going unanswered, or so it seems, as you wait day after day for a favorable report? To our benefit, this issue, among others, is addressed at John 11:1-45. It's the story of Lazarus.

Although it was Jesus' third instance of raising the dead (Mark 5:21-43; Luke 7:11-17), this one is the grand finale because Lazarus had been buried four days. Buried. Covered. Bound up in layers of cloth designed for the dead. The man is history, or so they thought about poor, ole Lazarus.

The story lets us know, I believe, that Jesus continues to raise the dead, literally—in more cases than are reported in the media—and figuratively: raising those spiritually "dead" in sin, raising those physically or mentally "covered" with disease, raising those emotionally "bound up" in dysfunctional habits, and raising those financially "buried" in bills.

If Jesus raised the dead back then, He can raise the dead today. But it appears that there's something *we* have to do to get this "raising from the dead" by our Savior into motion.

Notice that Jesus got others in on the act. He told the onlookers at the cave entrance to do something, and they obeyed. "Jesus said, 'Take away the stone'" (John 11:39 AMP). Although Martha, Lazarus' sister, at first complained how illogical that remark seemed to be (John 11:39)—as we might voice our "rational" complaints to something Jesus tells us to do—we see the command was followed: "So, they took away the stone" (John 11:41 AMP).

Shortly thereafter, Jesus "cried out with a loud voice" His famous line:

"Lazarus, come forth" (JOHN 11:43).

I believe our sacred text is letting us know as we do our part for a "bound up" individual, then God will do His part. That is, when we "take away the stone," then God raises them from the dead—whether it takes place instantly, in two days, two months, or twenty years.

How do we "take away the stone" on behalf of one needing a miracle? That's for God to reveal to each of us, and His methods are infinite. What is immediately coming to my mind are: intercessory prayer and practical helps.

In his first letter to Timothy, the apostle Paul writes, "I urge, then, first of all, that requests, prayers, intercession and thanksgiving be made for everyone . . ." (1 Tim. 2:1 NIV). Paul adds that favorable results are also in store for the one praying. That is, prayer enables the one praying to "lead a quiet and peaceable life in all godliness and reverence" (1 Tim. 2:1b). Plus, praying is "good and acceptable in the sight of God our Savior" (1 Tim. 2:2).

Practical helps are another way to "remove" another person's "stone." These "helps" play themselves out in numerous ways. One way: "Look after orphans and widows" (James 1:27 NIV).

Furthermore, it's been my experience that "the stone" often has to do with some aspect of purifying my own heart—as mentioned at James 4:8—and even calling me to be miserable and mourn and weep over my sins (James 4:9). While that doesn't sound like much fun, the long-range results are worth it. It's "the effective, fervent prayer of a *righteous*" one that gets the results (James 5:16 NKJV, emphasis added). So, I have to get the sin—such as unbelief (Matt. 13:58) or "a stony heart" (Ezek. 11:19, 36:26)—out of my own life before I can expect miraculous results from our God for a "bound up" individual, whether that be someone else *or* myself.

One might ask, though, "Why did God show favor on Lazarus? What about Larry, Laura, or Linda? They're just as much children of God as Lazarus. And haven't righteous others been praying up a storm for them? And doing all sorts of kind deeds for them? Why are *they* still bound up?"

In other words, how come God showed favor on Lazarus and not on a host of others in the same cave in the same condition?

In his first letter to the Corinthians, Paul acknowledges, "For now we see in a mirror, dimly. . . Now I know in part" (1 Cor. 13:12 NKJV). We don't have all the answers this side of heaven. And our unanswered questions seem to beg us, as believers, to see through the unsentimental eye of faith, and avoid the tendency to run away from God when we don't understand why God allows things like prolonged suffering and evil. As American writer Flannery O'Connor (1925-1964) cautions us, ". . . once you have discredited His goodness, you are done with Him."

Additional insight comes from Joni Eareckson Tada, who became a quadriplegic forty years ago after a diving accident. She writes in *The God I Love: A Lifetime of Walking with Jesus*:

> Lord, your no answer to physical healing meant yes to a deeper healing—a better one. Your answer has bound me to other believers and taught me so much about myself. It's purged sin from my life, it's strengthened my commitment to you, forced me to depend on your grace. Your wiser, deeper answer has stretched my hope, refined my faith, and helped me to know you better. And you are good. You are so good.

When Lazarus comes out of the tomb, Jesus tells the family and friends to take action, once again, on behalf of Lazarus as we saw at John 11:39. Jesus instructs them, "Take off the grave clothes and let him go" (John 11:44 NIV). And once more, the gathered throng obeyed. By design, this supernatural feat was not a solo act by our Savior. His creation—loved ones of a man bound up, buried and dead for four days—took an active part in the miracle, as they obeyed what Jesus told them to do.

Needless to say, Lazarus needed a little help from his friends: his Son of God/Son of Man friend Jesus and his earthly family and friends. And he got it in Bethany—big time.

I believe the same can happen today in our villages. That long-awaited prayer request might not be answered exactly how or when we want it to be answered. But a twenty-first century miracle, comparable to being raised from the dead, can become a precious reality.

As we ask God to tell us what "the stone" is in the situation of one needing a miracle, and then go about removing it with what God reveals to us—even if that means dealing with something unpleasant in our own lives—the results are in-for-the-making of some kind of miracle, for "Jesus Christ is the same yesterday and today and forever" (Heb. 13:8).

37

Take My Baby Jesus

(Matt. 2:13-14; John 1:29; 1 John 4:9-10)

Take my baby Jesus
Away from King Herod.
Take my baby Jesus
To Egypt, to safety,
To higher ground.
Take my baby Jesus.
For my baby Jesus
Takes my sins away.

Thank God It's Sunday

It's a good thing to go to church.

I'm reminded of a painting, "Sunday Morning," by American illustrator Norman Rockwell (1894-1978). The mother and three kids, in their Sunday best, march past the pajama-clad dad, slumped over in a chair, newspaper in hand with a look on his face that would suggest maybe he should be going to church, too.

That takes me to a day several years ago when I was prompted to look at Sunday in a different fashion. One Friday morning, as a secretary at a ministry, I casually asked my employer, "Aren't you glad it's Friday?" Without missing a beat, he replied, "Yeah. It's two days 'til Sunday."

Now that was not exactly what I had in mind insofar as *my* definition of "TGIF"—"Thank God it's Friday." Definitely, my boss had a holier perspective, reframing the weekend in a totally different light.

Saying "Thank God it's Sunday," with corresponding action, is indeed the way to go, as we see in Isaiah 58:

> "If because of the Sabbath, you turn your foot from doing your
> own pleasure on My holy day, and call the Sabbath a delight,
> the holy day of the LORD honorable, and honor it, desisting
> from your own ways, from seeking your own pleasure and
> speaking your own word, then you will take delight in the
> LORD, and I will make you ride on the heights of the earth; and
> I will feed you with the heritage of Jacob your father, for the
> mouth of the LORD has spoken" (ISA. 58:13-14).

In the above passage, I note the term, "turn your foot" (v. 13). The Lord knows the temptation to stay at home on Sunday morning, rather than make a literal turn toward honoring His holy day, such as getting ready for church and turning our feet toward the church doors.

Also, there's our attitude to consider. God wants us to "call the Sabbath a delight," not to ignore it, not to dread it, not to treat it like any other day of the week. The Sabbath is special, set apart, and holy. And I believe God wants us to say something like this:

> Thank You, Lord, that it's Your holy day. I delight in this
> Sabbath day. I am honored to spend the day with You, Lord. I
> will respect Your day and focus on You, Lord, seeking Your
> pleasure and speaking Your Word on Your holy day.

When our hearts and minds reach that point—and God is such a discerner of not only what we say and do, but also what we think in the depth of our hearts (Heb. 4:12; John 1:1)—there are benefits in store. That is, (1) when we refrain from doing and saying "our own thing," (2) when we consider the Sabbath "a delight," (3) when we treat the Sabbath with honor, and (4) respect the Lord's Day with our actions, not discount it by pursuing other things, then God will reward us.

How will God reward us?

What's in it for us?

What do we gain when we observe the Sabbath with the dignity that God has given it?

The Lord becomes a delight! That's a promise from God. He will supernaturally see to it that "you will take delight in the LORD" (Isa. 58:14). We don't have to manufacture the feelings. We will see the Lord in a more healthy and holy light. We will be changed. We will be blessed. For instance, over the years the passage, "For your Maker is your husband" (Isa. 54:5 NKJV) has taken on new meaning that comforts and sustains me more so than in earlier seasons in my life. And the list of God's blessings goes on and on . . . as we come to the point of honoring His day, like it's a weekly holiday. And other things get put aside for the Lord on His holy day.

Unquestionably, the passage from Isaiah lets us know the Sabbath is God's "holy day," as does one of the Ten Commandments: "Observe the Sabbath day by keeping it holy, as the LORD your God has commanded you" (Deut. 5:12 NLT).

Matthew Henry says there is "a beauty of holiness" upon the Lord's Day. "It is ancient, and its antiquity is its honor." And "we put honor upon the day when we give honor to Him that instituted it, and to whose honor it is dedicated."

In other words, as Matthew Henry comments, it's good to "make religion the business of the day."

Yet, we don't have to go overboard and get legalistic about the Lord's Day. Jesus himself did good deeds on the Sabbath (Luke 6:1-10), at one point even asking the Pharisees, "Is it lawful to do good or to do harm on the Sabbath, to save a life or to destroy it?" (Luke 6:9). That is sound advice; that is godly wisdom: to arrange our activities in a way that hinders as little as possible our giving honor to the Lord's Day.

Folks, *it's worth it* to have an honorable perspective of the Sabbath.

"Sunday Morning" by Norman Rockwell appeared on the cover of *The Saturday Evening Post* on May 16, 1959. I suppose the illustrator (whose "work has been reproduced more often than Michelangelo, Picasso and Rembrandt put together") must have known the dilemma we face: to stay at home or go to church on Sunday morning.

I would like to imagine our stay-at-home pajama-clad dad happens to turn to the religion section of the newspaper in his hands and finds this message:

And let us not neglect our meeting together, as some people do,
but encourage and warn each other, especially now that the day
of his [Jesus'] coming back again is drawing near
(HEB. 10:25 NLT).

And may the gentleman then be prompted, by the Holy Spirit, to "turn his foot" in the direction of church, making it on time for the second service, now that he's too late for the first. After all, would he rather be slumped over in a chair at home on Sunday morning, or begin a spiritual adventure that God promises, upon the aforementioned conditions being met, will make him "ride on the heights of the earth" (Isa. 58:14).

The C.O.S. Club

Are you a member of the C.O.S. Club? If not, I believe I understand why. The dues are steep and the obligations time-consuming. But those who belong tell me the benefits far exceed the costs involved.

What is the C.O.S. Club? Let me offer a hint. We become members when we dive into, or dog-paddle through, what novices in recovery call "the dreaded inventory." C.O.S. stands for: Confession of Sins. Its primary purpose is to take a look at caustic conduct, character defect, and toxic thought; then call it what it is: sin.

Here's seventeenth century philosopher, poet Thomas Traherne's take on its impact:

> A little grit in the eye destroyeth the sight of the very heavens,
> and a little malice or envy a world of joys. One wry principle in
> the mind is of infinite consequence.

There are several recovery organizations throughout our land. Furthermore, these venues, with five-star ratings in wisdom, tell us confession of sins is worth every penny. They add that making a moral inventory of ourselves and admitting our wrongs to another eventually turns into delight, like one's putting down a too-heavy suitcase, sighing with relief, and deliberately choosing not to pick it up again. In Christian circles, this is called repentance.

Participation in the C.O.S. Club is biblical. As Madeleine L'Engle writes in *Walking on Water*, it helps us to unlearn "the dirty devices of this world, which would dull our imaginations, cut away our creativity." Potential club members may check out the "bylaws":

Confess your sins to one another, and pray for one another so that you may be healed (JAMES 5:16).

Two are better than one because they have a good return for their work: If one falls down, his friend can help him up. But pity the man who falls and has no one to help him up! (ECCLES. 4:9-10 NIV).

If we confess our sins, [God] is faithful and righteous to forgive us our sins and to cleanse us from all unrighteousness (1 JOHN 1:9).

[As you draw near to God] be deeply penitent and grieve, even weep [over your disloyalty]. Let your laughter be turned to grief and your mirth to dejection and heartfelt shame [for your sins] (JAMES 4:9 AMP).

Humble yourselves—feeling very insignificant—in the presence of the Lord, and He will exalt you—He will lift you up and make your lives significant (JAMES 4:10 AMP).

O the bliss of those whose hearts are broken for the world's suffering and for their own sin, for out of their sorrow they will find the joy of God! (WILLIAM BARCLAY COMMENT ON MATT. 5:4).

Perhaps the most humble remark in the Bible belongs to a wayward boy telling his daddy, "Father, I have sinned against heaven and against you. I am no longer worthy to be called your son" (Luke 15:21 NIV). I pause over that confession, in grateful view of the celebration that follows (Luke 15:22-24).

We all need restitution: to make good after missing the mark; after treating someone with disrespect (a sin of commission); after failing to do a good deed when prompted by the Holy Spirit (a sin of omission).

After all, the Good Book tells us the essence of true religion is "to visit orphans and widows in their distress, and to keep oneself unstained by the world" (James 1:27). So I ask myself two questions:

Will I get my mind off myself and reach out to someone who feels like, or literally is, an orphan or widow in distress?

Will I keep myself unstained by the world?

So, here's looking at me, kids, in my "sackcloth and ashes" (Isa. 58:5; Matt. 11:21). Confession of sins is my top priority. God wants me to confess: Not with a sense of anxiety or fear, but with "a broken and a contrite heart," because that is what He "will not despise" (Ps. 51:17). With the eyes of faith, may I see the benefits on the other side: cleansing, healing, peace, significance, joy, loyalty—and royalty.

Think about it: The Almighty God allowing His One and Only Son, Jesus, "the loveliest life in all the world" (Barclay), totally without sin (1 Pet. 2:22; 1 John 3:5), taking upon himself the sins of the world. This is Jesus, the faithful one, keeping His promise and sending the Holy Spirit (John 14:16) to guide us through "the confusions and complications of life" (L'Engle). This is Jesus, the famous one, seated at the right hand of God (Heb. 1:5, 13), acting as "a high priest, holy, innocent, undefiled" (Heb. 7:26). And what is Jesus doing? Praying for you and me (Heb. 7:25).

Is it prime time to humbly and honestly confess the poverty and pollution within my soul, in appreciation for these sacrificial gifts?

Behold what manner of love
the Father has bestowed on us,
that we should be called children of God!
And everyone who has this hope in Him
purifies himself, just as He is pure
(1 John 3:1a, 3 NKJV).

The Common Good

Now there are varieties of gifts, but the same Spirit. And there
are varieties of ministries, and the same Lord. There are varieties of effects, but the same God who works all things in all
persons. But to each one is given the manifestation of the
Spirit for the common good (1 Cor. 12:4-7).

As the verse above powerfully proclaims, there are varieties of gifts,
ministries, and effects in the body of Christ. And each member of the
body has a function "for the common good," with positive effects when
the parts are working well together. This function is not mere duty. It's
a God thing. It is the manifestation of the Holy Spirit—"that is, the evidence, the spiritual illumination of the Spirit—for good and profit" (1
Cor. 12:7 AMP).

Before David set out to fight the giant Goliath, King Saul "put a
bronze helmet" on David's head, and "he clothed him with armor" (1
Sam. 17:38). Saul's "hand-me-down" clothes quickly proved to be the
wrong mode of operation for David, who told Saul that he could not
go into battle against Goliath with Saul's armor, for "I have not tested
them" (1 Sam. 17:39).

We will recall the successful outcome of David's battle with Goliath
(1 Sam. 17:50) after David wisely chose his own personal, tested style
of armor: a slingshot with five smooth stones (1 Sam. 17:40). Saul's
heavy armor was a hindrance, rather than a help.

That reminds me several years ago when I was seeking a clearer definition of my role in the body of Christ. God answered that prayer—at least a portion of it—in 1995 after I broke my right thumb. Several weeks later, I am reasonably certain that the Lord told me that I am "a broken right thumb to the body of Christ."

God took my literal broken, right thumb and moved it to the metaphorical, as though He were speaking to the poet within my soul. To understand this supposed word from the Lord, I noticed what the Lord said and what He did not say. And I checked to see if it lined up with Scripture.

I believe His exact words in 1995 were: "You are a broken right thumb to the body of Christ." God's statement related to one thumb: "*a* broken right thumb." I am one individual—with one and only one member's role to fulfill "to the body of Christ." I'm not to be "*all* thumbs." That would frustrate me—and others. And I'm not to be "all things to all people." That would exhaust me and cripple my bearing fruit (John 15:8).

The Lord said I am "a *broken* right thumb." I discern God wants me to be broken rather than prideful, humble rather than haughty. The Bible speaks of brokenness in a favorable light. "It is better to be of a humble [broken] spirit with the lowly, than to divide the spoil with the proud" (Prov. 16:19). Or, "The sacrifices of God are a broken spirit; a broken and a contrite heart, O God, Thou wilt not despise" (Ps. 51:17 KJV). Or, how relevant is this one: "Let the bones which You have broken rejoice" (Ps. 51:8b).

By God's definition, I am "a broken *right* thumb . . ." The Word of God often speaks poetically with phrases like "the *right* hand of God," as in Hebrews 1:13. Similarly, right is the root word of "righteousness."

God did not say a broken right hand or arm. And He did not say an ear, an eye, or foot (1 Cor. 12:15-16). And He made no mention of being a head (1 Cor.12:21). That is, I am not to be *more* than God has wired me to be. That would prove of little or no benefit—like young David trying to wear King Saul's armor to fight Goliath.

And I'm not to be *less* than God has wired me to be. For example, God did not say I am a broken, right cuticle. That, too, would prove of little or no benefit—like David fighting Goliath with a twig, rather than David's tested slingshot.

God did not say I am a broken, right hang-nail. That sounds more like the condemning voice of the devil, who accuses us "before our God day and night" (Rev. 12:10). Just the thought of a voice in my head calling me a "hang-nail." Nix on that.

God did not say I am "a broken right thumb" to any ministry where I was employed in 1995, nor to any specific church, but "*to the body of Christ.*" If and when I'm operating in any form or fashion other than "a broken right thumb to the body of Christ," I believe I am out of God's Will—either making too much of myself or too little of myself.

Have you ever tried to start the ignition of a car with a broken right thumb? My inability to turn the ignition key with a broken right thumb in 1995 led me to a heightened appreciation of a healthy right thumb—and the positive effects of a good, right thumb working together with the fingers of a good, right hand and arm.

"For the body is not one member, but many" (1 Cor. 12:14).

Do you remember the children's song, "Dry Bones"? It begins: "The foot bone's connected to the ankle bone; the ankle bone's connected to the leg bone." And the bone connections continue up the frame's ladder until "the neck bone's connected to the head bone."

"Dry Bones" also includes the lyrics, "Ezekiel connected dem dry bones. Oh, hear the word of the Lord." The song is taken from Ezekiel 37:1-6, where God brought the prophet Ezekiel to a valley of bones. God asked Ezekiel if these bones could live. Ezekiel responded in the affirmative, and then God told him to prophesy over "Dem Dry Bones."

I believe Ezekiel's prophesy is a promise for the body of Christ. Not only are we to "hear the word of the Lord," we are to put His word into practice, and connect with our gifts and ministries for the common good and the glory of God.

> "Behold, I [the LORD] will cause breath to enter you that you may come to life. And I will put sinews on you, make flesh grow back on you, cover you with skin, and put breath in you that you may come alive; and you will know that I am the LORD" (EZEK. 37:5-6).

The Leaning Tower

Have you ever seen one of the seven wonders of the world? Thanks to the generosity of my parents, I was able to tour Western Europe between my junior and senior year of college. Among other memories, I remember the day our tour bus made a sharp right turn toward a level green lawn known as the "Field of Miracles" (*Campo dei Miracoli*). Our Swiss-born tour guide stood in front of the bus, pointing out one of the wonders of the world. There it was, right in front of me, as I dropped my jaw in astonishment: The Leaning Tower of Pisa. In all of its beauty, majesty, and mystery: *La Torre Pendente di Pisa*.

On that eventful summer day, I hiked the winding steps of the Cathedral's 185-foot bell tower for a bird's-eye view of Pisa, Italy. That was 1971, when I was 21. Unfortunately, since 1988, the eight-story Tower has been closed to the public because of concern over the increased inclination, which is about a 10-degree angle, the top being 17 feet further over than was originally intended.

Needless to say, I fondly remember seeing this most famous of medieval bell towers, which reminds me of another "leaning tower" I came across during the course of a Bible study by Beth Moore. In *Believing God*, she writes:

> By faith Jacob, when he was dying, blessed each of Joseph's
> sons, and worshiped as he *leaned* on the top of his staff"
> (HEB. 11:21 NIV, EMPHASIS ADDED).

Maybe it's because I'm past the half-century mark that I find my thoughts turning more frequently to the limits of my "earthly tent." Maybe it's because I have a little degeneration in my back, and I literally lean more than I used to. Or maybe it's because, as songwriter Bill Withers sang in the 1970s, "We all need somebody to lean on." Regardless of the reasons, I was touched to read that Jacob "leaned on the top of his staff" "when he was dying" and he "worshiped" (Heb. 11:21 NIV).

Think of the different things Jacob could have done prior to death. He could have become bitter. He could have withdrawn in defeat. He could have turned to excessive drinking or drugs. He could have spoken words that curse, rather than bless (James 3:10). He could have given up all signs of exercising faith.

Jacob persevered (Rev. 3:10). Jacob acted responsibly at the finish line (Gen. 47:27-31). Jacob fulfilled his obligations to his family. He "blessed each of Joseph's sons" (Heb. 11:21). He even spoke prophetically to his sons (Gen. 48:17-49:1-33). Jacob demonstrated faith, which is "being sure of what we hope for and certain of what we do not see" (Heb. 11:1 NIV).

Jacob worshiped God.

I imagine Jacob "leaned on the top of his staff" because he was frail and needed support. And a "staff" is a symbol of God's guidance and strength. Think of the numerous times a shepherd's staff appears in the Bible, such as Psalm 23. In other words, Jacob "leaned" on God during his weakest hour.

Aren't we, at times, too frail to stand up on our own without support: whether it's a cane or wheelchair that we need for physical support; a smile or a kind word for emotional support; a Christmas bonus or retirement package for financial support; a prayer or verse in the Bible for spiritual support? Regardless of the terrain, what do we lean on when we are weak and weary?

Jacob *leaned* on God. Jacob relied on God. Jacob depended on our Lord.

And that root word *lean* appears in different forms elsewhere in the Bible, as in these two scriptures:

Trust in the LORD with all thine heart, and *lean* not unto thine own understanding (PROV. 3:5 KJV, EMPHASIS ADDED).

Now there was *leaning* on Jesus' bosom one of his disciples, whom Jesus loved (JOHN 13:23 KJV, EMPHASIS ADDED).

Not only did Jacob lean on his staff; he worshiped God. The importance of worship is prominently stated in these two scriptures:

"But an hour is coming, and now is, when the true worshipers will worship the Father in spirit and truth; for such people the Father seeks to be His worshipers" (JOHN 4:23).

Worship the LORD in the beauty of holiness (PS. 29:2 KJV).

I'm inspired to see Jacob's "increased inclination" toward God before taking his final breath, which our tour guide might describe this way:

Tourists, up ahead to your right, just past a level stretch of grass called "The Field of Faith," is the "Piazza of Hebrews 1121," as noted in your Guidebook. Here we see the architectural integrity of "The Leaning Tower": a tired and tried man of faith named Jacob (or Israel), leaning on top of his staff prior to his death and worshiping God, as Jacob's God was his "Tower of Strength."

The Light Touch

(Mark 5:35-43; Luke 8:49-56)

So many people are crying inside
the house of a synagogue ruler.
A twelve year old is dead.

Jesus speaks to the crowd,
"The child is not dead. She's asleep."

They don't believe.

He proves His point:
"Little girl! I tell you to get up!"

Now you'd think, after such a feat,
Jesus would command everyone,
"Bow down! Worship Me!
Repent of your unbelief."

Wrong.

Slowly, matter-of-fact
He turns around and tells them,

"Give her something to eat."

I imagine
the little girl
smiles
at the man called Jesus
and cleans her plate.

True North

"What is truth?" asks Pontius Pilate, after Jesus had told him, "For this I have come into the world, to bear witness to the truth" and "everyone who is of the truth hears My voice" (John 18:37). Furthermore, Jesus had answered the question, "What is truth?" in an earlier conversation with Thomas, when Jesus said, "I am the way, and the truth, and the life" (John 14:6).

Truth is "the unveiled reality lying at the basis of, and agreeing with, an appearance; the manifested, the veritable essence of matter." It is "in opposition to the worship of false idols" and to "one doing foul, trivial, evil things." Greek scholar Spiros Zodhiates describes truth as "purity from all error or falsehood."

To follow Jesus Christ is to follow truth—"unveiled reality." But how do we follow truth this day, this hour, this moment? The Word says that "when the Spirit of truth comes, He will guide you into all truth" (John 16:13 NLT). Not partial truth, not falsehood, but all truth. This is a promise to remember.

At times I wonder if I'm in the will of God in certain aspects of my life. And God often leads me to others wiser than I am (Prov. 11:14) including Oswald Chambers who wrote in *Daily Thoughts for Disciples*:

> The Holy Spirit is God Almighty's gift if we simply become poor enough to ask for Him. . . . But when the Holy Spirit has come in, there is something we can do and God cannot do—we can obey Him. If we do not obey Him, we shall grieve Him.

I vividly remember a day over two decades ago when I grieved the Holy Spirit through disobedience (Eph. 4:30). It was a Thursday afternoon around 3 o'clock, and I was in the office by myself. All of a sudden I heard in my spirit, "Call your mother." I was not familiar with the voice of God "speaking" like this within my spirit. Erroneously, I resorted to my own reasoning—forgetting that God's ways are higher than my ways, and His thoughts than my thoughts (Isa. 55:9). I said to myself: "Good grief. Mother and Dad will be in town tomorrow night. I can talk with them then. Besides, it would be a long distance call." So, the Voice of God, which appeared like a sudden light bulb turning on in my head, I simply dismissed.

The next day, Friday, I learned that Mother and Dad's pug had been taken to the vet on Thursday morning for what was considered a routine surgery. And the dog died. Mother had gotten the vet's phone call at home that afternoon and, understandably, as Dad said, she was "pretty upset."

I asked Dad, "When did Mother get the news from the vet?"

"Around 3:00 o'clock." The exact time God had spoken to my spirit. I missed out on a precious opportunity to console my own mother, and I grieved the Holy Spirit that Thursday afternoon.

In Alan Paton's novel, *Cry, A Beloved Country*, we find these remarks:

I shall no longer ask myself if this or that is expedient, but only if it is right. I shall do this, not because I am noble or unselfish, but because life slips away, and because I need for the rest of my journey a star that will not play false to me, a compass that will not lie.

The Holy Spirit is a holy-calibrated "compass that will not lie" (John 14:16-17, 26). And God does not play hide and seek with us as we seek His Will. God wants us to know His Will. But there are counterfeits that distract and distort; that attempt to cause us to stray from true north; to lose our bearings, to miss the mark, to find ourselves in a trap of conflict and confusion.

The main counterfeiter is the devil who "does not stand in the truth, because there is no truth in him." And whenever the devil "speaks a lie, he speaks from his own nature; for he is a liar, and the father of lies" (John 8:44).

Another counterfeiter taking us away from true north is a character Brennan Manning calls "the Imposter."

> Everyone's got one. It's "the slick, sick, and subtle impersonator of my true self." The persona craves to be liked, loved, approved, accepted, to fit in. "It's the self that refuses to accept that my true self, centered in Christ, is really more likeable, more attractive, and more real than the fallen self."

Sometimes we think we're plain-as-day right; and only "the Spirit of truth" (John 16:13) can change our stubborn way of thinking, as in this little verse called "Math My Way" from *Lunch Money and Other Poems About School*:

> Two plus two is twenty-two.
> It's plain as day that this is true.
> But teacher says she's very sure
> That two plus two adds up to four.

Pontius Pilate asked Jesus, "What is truth?" (John 18:38). Then, Pilate walked away from standing in the presence, the "veritable essence" of Truth.

Like Pontius Pilate, will we walk away from "unveiled reality" and go elsewhere with our "slick, sick, and subtle" fabrications? Will we insist "Two plus two is twenty-two"? Will we refuse to recognize and combat the lies of Satan? Will we lift up banners of false reasoning and misplaced confidence higher than the supremacy of holy Scripture?

Like magnetic and electronic devices distort a compass from pointing to true north, will we be led astray by stuff—"the cares of this age, the deceitfulness of riches, and the lusts of other things"? (Mark 4:19 KJV).

Or will we, as followers of Jesus Christ, earnestly seek for the rest of our journey "a star that will not play false," "a compass that will not lie"?

As we accept and grow into our "true self, centered in Christ"—"more likeable, more attractive, and more real than the fallen self"—may we take hold of God's promise: that the Holy Spirit will guide us into all truth (John 16:13). For true north always points to Jesus Christ as "the way, and the truth, and the life" (John 14:6a).

Truly, Truly

When Lionel Richie appeared on stage at Barton Coliseum in Little Rock, Arkansas, over twenty-five years ago, my twin sister and I tried to guess what would be his opening song. While I have forgotten Brenda's prediction, I distinctly remember when I guessed "Truly," she immediately replied the concert would end with "Truly," not begin with it. Unlike other occasions, I was right this time. Lionel's opening number was "Truly."

When our Lord and Savior had something very important to say, He would begin His remarks not with one "Truly" but two. This is comparable to reading sentences that are underscored, in **bold print**, in ALL CAPS, or followed by an exclamation point! We are to take note to what Jesus is about to say is: "Extra, Extra: Read All About It!"

In the Book of John, Jesus prefaces His remarks with "Truly, truly, I say to you . . ." twenty-five times. Of these very important remarks, I sought to answer the question: What does Jesus want us to know more than anything else? While I'm no biblical scholar, I made a few observations from the last book of the four gospels.

The first time Jesus said, "Truly, truly, I say to you," He was speaking to Nathanael, whom Jesus had earlier said there was no fault in this man (John 1:47). (Can you think of any higher compliment to receive from the Lord of lords?) The verse reads: "Truly, truly, I say to you [Nathanael], you will see the heavens opened and the angels of God ascending and descending on the Son of Man" (John 1:51). Beth Moore notes this verse from the New Testament is linked with the Old

Testament at Genesis 28:12 to accent: "God is the only connector of earth and heaven" and "Jesus is Jacob's ladder."

In John 3:1-21, Nicodemus is taught that Jesus and His disciples "speak of what we know" and these are not "earthly things," but "heavenly things" (John 3:11-12). Jesus' focus was and remains: "whoever *believes* will in Him have eternal life" (John 3:15, emphasis added). In fact, the eternal life (or "new birth") theme is saturated with "truly, truly" (John 3:3, 5, 11)—in response to Nicodemus' thoughtful questions (John 3:2, 4, 9).

Jesus repeats the "eternal life" theme in John 5, speaking now to a group of people, rather than one to one: "Truly, truly, I say to you, he who hears My word, and *believes* [God, the Father] who sent Me, has eternal life, and does not come into judgment, but has passed out of death into life" (John 5:24, emphasis added). Then again in John 6: "Truly, truly, I say to you, he who *believes* has eternal life" (John 6:47, emphasis added), also known as abundant life (John 10:10b).

What is the main theme of the "truly, truly" passages? Believe Jesus.

To help us believe, Jesus reveals His character and His conduct. Jesus was not the independent type, nor was He codependent. (God-directed actions bring joy, peace, and righteousness: Rom. 14:17; Isa. 32:17. Self-directed or codependent actions do not.) Jesus follows the lead of His Father, emphatically telling us He could "do nothing of Himself"— nothing on His own initiative (John 5:19, 30). Jesus obeyed His Superior Authority. I ask myself, "Whose lead will I follow today?" (John 12:26).

Jesus impresses upon us His knowledge of human nature. He compares committing sin with slavery and following Him with freedom (John 8:34-36). Elsewhere, Jesus cautions us to watch our motives: "Truly, truly, I say to you, you seek Me . . . because you ate of the loaves and were filled" (John 6:26). Jesus calls us to a higher place: "Do not work for the food which perishes, but for the food which endures to eternal life" (John 6:27a).

Jesus' emphasis on His being "the true bread out of heaven" (John 6:32) is compared with the literal bread, manna, that fell from heaven during the days of Moses (Exodus 16:15). *The Quest Study Bible* comments that Jesus' "truly, truly" statement on eating and drinking "of the Son of Man" (John 6:53) is a passionate plea "to assimilate and allow Him into every aspect of our lives."

Metaphors abound: Jesus is "the bread of life" (John 6:48) and "the good shepherd," not "a hired hand" (John 10:11-12). Note another: "Truly, truly, I say to you, I am the door of the sheep" (John 10:7). *Merriam-Webster's Collegiate Dictionary* says a door is a means of access or participation; a means "by which an entry is closed or opened." Jesus is the door, and we are His sheep.

Jesus emphasizes conditional blessings and promises: "Truly, truly, I say to you, *if* anyone keeps My word he will never see death" (John 8:51, emphasis added). Another one: "Truly, truly, I say to you, *if* you ask the Father for anything in My name, He will give it to you" (John 16:23, emphasis added; see also John 15:16). In other words, Jesus definitely, definitely wants us to know what He is capable of doing for us from Creator to creation *if* we will obey His Word.

Is it time to walk in these great spiritual truths? Is it time to believe Jesus?

In closing, I've got a question for any musically-inclined reader. I'm thinking of a song. Lionel Richie wrote the words and the music in 1980, and it appears on the compact disc: "Commodores: All the Great Love Songs." Lionel is the lead singer on this gospel song, and the title is closely associated with the last three words of 1 John 4:8.

What is the song? **"JESUS IS LOVE!"**

I think we (want-to-be biblical scholars and musical fans alike) could easily preface that with: "Truly, Truly . . ."

Unraveled and Untitled

Are we not prone to say, "We are fine," even when we are not so fine? After all, "fine" is what others want us to be; "fine" is what we want to be. So, we say, "We are fine" even when "un-fine" registers inside our body, mind, or soul.

Within community, a glimpse of "un-fine" eventually emerges. Trust develops between two or more individuals, and it becomes safe to say, "Not everything is in tip-top shape." Like a flower takes time to bloom, so does trust. Some people drop out of community before this happens. Preoccupation with other things is too entrenched; time is precious; pain is great. But with tenacity, trust reveals its first bud: we offer a glimpse of our un-fineness to another soul. This initial unraveling often comes in small ways. Something minute is revealed: a rained-out game, an over-cooked roast, a broken fingernail. But this is a step. And God honors steps, even awkward baby-steps.

Like holding a heavenly kaleidoscope, God moves in multiple ways to show His fine design to His sons and daughters. To the introvert, who struggles in community, God's revelation of himself may be quite different than to the extrovert. God knows us through and through. He knows how to communicate with us, consistent with our personality. After all:

God is passionate about His relationship with us
(EXOD. 34:14 NLT).

He cares for us (1 PET. 5:7).

He yearns for us (JAMES 4:5).

His thoughts toward us are precious (Ps. 139:17).

His faithfulness is great (LAM. 3:22-23).

There are two majestic themes God has placed within the landscape of the human heart; two great hungers within our soul: truth and beauty. One is enlightened by truth and renewed by beauty. In "Ode on a Grecian Urn," John Keats wrote, "Beauty is truth, truth beauty." I think those words were inspired by God. The Bible tells us God is the God of truth (Isa. 65:16), and His truth makes us free (John 8:32). Furthermore, everything God made He called "good" (Gen. 1:4, 10, 12, 21, 25, 31), which I believe is synonymous with "beautiful."

When one comes to the Holy Father through His Son, Jesus Christ (1 Tim. 2:5), one may see, as though for the first time, beauty in the rustle of yellow-green leaves set in motion by a gentle breeze. One may see, as though for the first time, brown, black and white woven like a rich tapestry on the wings of a sparrow. One may see, as though for the first time, the early morning fog over the red banks of a winding river. Beauty in the full-body stretch of a football player in mid-air as he catches an overthrown pass; beauty in the light and delicate hops on pointe of a ballerina; beauty in the power of the brass in Dvořák's "From The New World" symphony; beauty in the community of violins in Vivaldi's "The Four Seasons."

Like a new leaf that turns, something awakens within the soul who becomes one with their Creator (1 Cor. 6:17): something deeply significant, abundant, and sweet: an unraveling of beauty; an epiphany of truth. At that moment, one can hardly help but think of their favorite things. Whatever is pure, lovely and admirable . . . (Phil. 4:8): yellow roses; red poinsettias; the first robin in spring; wind chimes; the texture of lace; the taste of pumpkin pie; the laughter of friends; the "fragrance of Christ" (2 Cor. 2:14-15).

In order to fully know what truth and beauty are, God also shows us what they are not. Beauty is belittled. Boundaries are breached. Calm turns to storm. Trust turns to distrust. Truth is divided. Yet, there is purpose: How would we know light if we did not know darkness? Joy if we did not know sorrow? How would we long for "a better country—a heavenly one" (Heb. 11:16 NIV) if things were picture-perfect on earth? The contrasting elements of truth and beauty, our sovereign God allows on an as-needed basis.

During periods that Thomas Paine describes as "times that try men's souls," God's character does not change (Mal. 3:6). He remains the God of love (1 John 4:8). He remains a good God (Nah. 1:7) in seasons of redemptive suffering (Hosea 2:14; Rom. 5:3-5; 2 Cor. 12:7-9; James 1:2-3).

And one day, our Holy God will transport His faithful sons and daughters—whom He calls "overcomers"—to a reserved place of indescribable beauty; a rewarding place of family reunions; a spectacular place of supernatural truth. The choice location is called heaven (Matt. 25:34). Its alternate for the disinherited is called hell (Matt. 7:21; Mark 9:47-48; 2 Pet. 2:4).

Meanwhile, in the busyness or quiet of our earthly lives: through His Word, through worship, through prayer, through community, through all of His creation, God speaks. We listen. We respond—sometimes with His favor, sometimes without. He takes note (2 Chron. 16:9). He keeps records. He knows our future (Rev. 20:11-15). He knows our frame (Ps. 103:14).

Through the myriad of human experience, our Creator asks something from us. He does not need it. He does not demand it. He will not manipulate to get it. But He desires something from us. What do you think it is?

God is so good and so holy that the only thing He can work with, as our Creator, is something less than Him. Compared to God, we are less. We fall short of His glory (Rom. 3:23). We tremble in His presence (Isa. 6:4; Isa. 66:2; Phil. 2:12-13). Compared to God, aren't all of us un-fine? And He is supremely fine, divine, infinite, all knowing.

What does God want from us? He wants our brokenness (Matt. 11:28; Luke 19:10). Because that is what He takes and turns, as holding an untitled masterpiece, reshapes and reframes, enabling us to relive in the truth and beauty of holiness (Ps. 29:2 NKJV). And that is how I define being born again (John 3:3; Rom. 10:9-13).

Printed in the United States
91976LV00002B/103-198/A

9 781932 124934